# Contents

# Students at Risk

*Solutions to Classroom Challenges*

Cheryll Duquette

Pembroke Publishers Limited

*To my parents, Irene and Bill,*
*who encouraged me to pursue*
*my dreams;*
*to Karras and Anders, whose*
*patience and inspiration have*
*been appreciated; and*
*to John, whose support has*
*been unending*

© **2001 Pembroke Publishers**
538 Hood Road
Markham, Ontario, Canada L3R 3K9
www.pembrokepublishers.com

Distributed in the U.S. by Stenhouse Publishers
477 Congress Street
Portland, ME 04101
www.stenhouse.com

We acknowledge the financial support of the Government of Canada through the Book Publishing Industry Development Program (BPIDP) for our publishing activities.

National Library of Canada Cataloguing in Publication Data

Duquette, Cheryll
    Students at risk : solutions to classroom challenges

Includes bibliographical references and index.
ISBN 1-55138-135-4

    1. Handicapped children—Education.
2. Mainstreaming in education. I. Title.

LC3965.D86 2001        371.9'046        C2001-901392-2

Cover photo taken in Jim Dart's class at Wells Street Public School.

Editor:          Kate Revington
Cover Design:    John Zehethofer
Cover Photo:     Ajay Photographics
Typesetting:     Jay Tee Graphics Ltd.

Printed and bound in Canada
9 8 7 6 5 4 3 2 1

# Preface

As professionals, we all want to do more than just presenting the curriculum. We want to ensure that all of our students are learning as much as possible in our classrooms. However, even if you are an experienced teacher, you may find your job more challenging than in the past. That is likely because you must deal with the inclusion of students with exceptionalities. These students are the children who have been formally identified as having a learning disability, behavioral/emotional disorder, sensory impairment, developmental disability, or physical impairment, or giftedness. You also have an ever-increasing number of children who are at risk of having academic or behavior problems in school. And, of course, all of these students have special needs.

Many teachers have not had an opportunity to obtain training in working with children with exceptionalities. They feel frustrated at their seeming inability to effectively adapt their teaching and modify curriculum to meet the needs of exceptional students. If you are one of them, you will find that this book offers ways to teach students who have identified exceptionalities or who are suspected of having a disability, a behavior problem, or a gift.

*Students at Risk* is divided into two sections.

In Part A you will find an explanation of the process for working with children who are at risk of developing academic or behavior problems, but have not yet been identified. You will see how the process was applied to Andrew, Alex, and Erik, three *unidentified* elementary and junior high students whose teachers realized that they were at risk and provided accommodations for them. You will also read about the progress of these students as their teachers implemented plans of action and see how to work with others when developing a plan for a student.

Part B of this book is devoted to providing you with descriptions of various disabilities, behavior problems, and giftedness. Lists of characteristics shown by students with these exceptionalities are included so that you can check off those you observe over time. Your observations as a teacher may be the catalyst for the detection of an exceptionality, such as a learning disability or giftedness. Practical suggestions on how to work with a student who has an exceptionality are also presented, so that you may decide how to best accommodate the needs of a particular child. These recommended practices apply not only to those students who you suspect of having an exceptionality, but also to those who have already been formally identified. They may also be used with students who need remediation in a particular area, who have a minor behavior problem, or who may benefit from enrichment. Finally, a few reproducible pages are prepared for you so that they may be used immediately.

You *can* work effectively with the students who have disabilities, disruptive behaviors, and gifts. You just need to know the process of developing a plan of action and the tools to put it in place. This book will provide you with the process and the tools that will help you make a difference in the academic progress and social development of the children you teach.

# The Process of Working with Students with Disabilities, Behavior Problems, or Gifts

# CHAPTER 1

# Observing Students

We have all been in the situation where a student's performance or behavior caused us some concern. Perhaps a student seems to understand things orally, but can't express himself on paper. Maybe you have a student whose behaviors disrupt the learning of the other children. Or you wonder about a student in your classroom who grasps new concepts very quickly, is among the first in the class to complete her work, and usually has it done correctly. You may suspect that these students have a learning disability, a behavioral disorder, or a gift. And because the referral process usually takes months, even if the child were identified as having an exceptionality, he or she might no longer be in your class by the time an Individual Education Plan (IEP) is written. Nevertheless, you want to do your best for these students while they are with you, and you may have some ideas to help them.

What you need is a framework or process to help these students. One that works well consists of the following steps: (1) observing, (2) formulating goals, (3) developing strategies, and (4) implementing and reviewing the action plan. This framework is based on the classic process of problem solving which is widely used in administration.

In this chapter we will examine how to observe students, especially those who have not yet been identified as having an exceptionality.

## Know Your Students

One of the most important things you can do as a teacher is to know your students: their strengths, weaknesses, and interests. You may do this in several ways. Simply observe their classroom work and behaviors and keep formal and informal records. Examine the files in which are kept report cards, records of achievement testing, and so on. Pay particular attention to the comments made by previous teachers on the report cards. These will give you a sense about earlier achievement levels, work habits, and behaviors. The results of any psychological testing or medical examination will tell you about the child's intelligence, specific learning disabilities, the presence of AD/HD, or other exceptionalities. You might be surprised by what you discover. Perhaps a particular student tested as gifted, which may explain why she is finished the work

A student who is identified as having an exceptionality has undergone a formal assessment consisting of individual standardized tests that measure intelligence and other assessment methods related to the area of the suspected disability, disorder, impairment, or gift. A committee reviews the results of the tests and decides if the child has an exceptionality and what special accommodations are required. Then an Individual Education Plan (IEP) is prepared. An IEP is a legal document that states the strengths, needs, and ways to accommodate special needs. It is based on the results of the assessment and is written by the classroom teacher, the special education teacher, and sometimes the parent and child. The student's progress is noted and reviewed at least once a year, and the IEP is updated accordingly.

before everyone else and is filling in time by talking to others. Or, another student proves to have a hearing impairment, which may explain why he rarely seems to participate in group discussions or follows oral instructions.

Speak to the student, the parents, and previous teachers, as well. I have found that by about Grade 4 a child will be able to tell you why work is not being completed (e.g., *can't see the board, don't want to do the work and prefer to play with my pencil, don't understand the work, can't write what's in my head, can't copy very quickly, it's too easy*). Parents can also provide information about the child's previous progress, abilities, effective teaching techniques, home life, and so on. Previous teachers will likely be able to tell you about academic levels, interpersonal skills, classroom behaviors, and teaching techniques that worked for them.

You need to make observations and gather information about a student in order to determine the child's academic strengths and weaknesses, as well as extracurricular interests and activities. The weaknesses then translate into the goals for improvement.

You may be able to use a student's strengths to achieve the goals. As an example, I once taught a Grade 7 student who knew *everything* about 18-wheelers. That year, almost all of his creative writing was on the one subject he knew: trucks. Because he felt confident about the subject matter, he was able to accept my spelling and grammar corrections. Through the corrections and individual conferencing, we were able to improve his skill levels in those two areas.

The observations you make at the beginning of the process serve as the baseline of academic performance or behaviors so that you may measure improvement. Below are some ways to observe students.

## Academic Performance

### Elementary students

Record keeping is extremely important in making observations about a child's academic performance. Generally, you can use published checklists and anecdotal reports recorded in a private journal. In the primary grades, keep track of whether the work is completed and handed in. This may be done by checking off the child's name on a class list. You may also want to make some informal notes in a private journal about whether the child seems to understand the concepts. You will notice this through the written work that you correct every day, during class time as you teach the material, and when you circulate around the classroom while the students work on an assignment. While you circulate, you will observe who seems to be struggling to understand the instructions or concepts. You will also see who grasps the ideas easily and finishes the work well ahead of the others. As you make your observations over a period of time, for example, two to four weeks, notice how often work is incomplete, not understood, or completed accurately and quickly.

Note as well in which subject areas such work trends are occurring. For example, you may have a student whose oral reading and comprehension are not at grade level and who has difficulty with spelling and written expression. In this case, you would note the performance of the child in these three subject areas over a few weeks. The more specific your observations, the easier it will be to develop a plan for the child. For example, if the child struggles with oral reading, try to note the specific areas of difficulty, such as phonological awareness, phonics, decoding skills, omission of words, or insertion of words. Be discreet about making the observations. Note them during the oral reading sessions and record them using the published checklist that may accompany your reading series or that is distributed by your district. You might also consider recording observations in a private journal when the children are not in the classroom and keeping the journal in a locked cabinet.

You should also note the student's academic achievement. This may be done through teacher-made tests and assignments. Subject-based skill-development checklists that have been prepared by your board of education are another option. For oral reading, you may use word lists for a specific grade that are prepared by the publisher of the language texts. The child would read these words, and you would note those that were read correctly and those that were read incorrectly. For the words read incorrectly, note whether they were guesses or whether the child tried to sound them out. In the latter case, write what the child pronounced. For example, if the word was "mate" and the child pronounced "mat," write what was said beside the word that was pronounced incorrectly. When the child has finished reading the words, examine the words that were pronounced correctly and incorrectly to determine specific patterns. After examining the list, you may notice that the child knows short vowels, but not long vowels, for example. Be sure to make many observations over time to determine whether or not the child really does know the long vowel sounds. A single observation is insufficient because the child may not have been feeling well or may just have been inattentive. Track the child's performance in daily work and on tests and assignments for a few weeks.

As well, note *clusters* of difficulties, such as those in the language area: reading, spelling, and written expression. Note the child's speech and language development. Listen to pronunciation, vocabulary used, and sentence structure. You may notice difficulties in math, too, particularly in remembering the facts and procedures about how to do the operations involved in adding (such as carrying), subtracting (such as borrowing), multiplying, and dividing. Consider that a child who has difficulties with problem solving may also have problems with reading comprehension. Also note the motor skills of the child: fine motor, as shown in printing or writing; and gross motor, as in running, jumping, or climbing. Observe whether the child can organize his or her work, how long an attention span the child has developed, and what the level of social skill development is. You may want to use a Screening Checklist, such as appears on page 12, to record your observations. It provides a general guide for observing a student's development and skill levels. A reproducible version appears as an appendix.

# Screening Checklist

Name: _Patrick_  Grade: _4_  Date of Birth: _June 25, 1992_

## Language
- ❑ Oral Reading — *some hesitancy, doesn't pay attention to punctuation, slow pace, little intonation, reads a rehearsed passage better*
- ❑ Reading Comprehension — *can answer most fact and detail questions, some difficulty with main idea and inference, seems to understand more when listens to a tape and reads*
- ❑ Spelling — *weekly spelling tests are well done, everyday spelling is weaker, has trouble sounding out words, sequence of letters in middle and end of words is sometimes a problem*
- ❑ Written Expression — *can express sequential thought, ideas are usually expressed logically, does not put much effort into creative writing, applies punctuation and capitalization rules most of the time*
- ❑ Oral Expression — *extensive vocabulary, no articulation problems, expresses ideas logically and sequentially, volunteers answers regularly*
- ❑ Oral Comprehension — *follows directions, understands passages better when read orally*

## Math
- ❑ Concepts — *good understanding: numbers, operations, measurements, patterns, geometry*
- ❑ Facts — *knows +, −, ×, and ÷ to 12*
- ❑ Problem Solving — *better understanding of what is asked when problem is read orally*

## Motor Skills
- ❑ Fine Motor — *handwriting is slower, well formed (cursive and manuscript), stays within lines*
- ❑ Gross Motor — *able to throw and catch, maneuver a ball with right and left feet*

## Work Skills
- ❑ Organization — *locates materials when required, organizes own homework, able to anticipate time limits*
- ❑ Attention Span — *can usually focus on work until completion, not easily distracted except when reading*
- ❑ Social Skills — *works well with others, plays with a small group of same-sex friends, accepting of authority*

## Other
- — *far-point copying is slower than near-point copying, can reproduce shapes on paper*
- — *doesn't seem to do much reading for pleasure*
- — *was on the school soccer and cross-country running teams*

## Summary
*Math, motor skills, work skills, oral skills (receptive and expressive), and writing are average to above average.*
*Reading and spelling need reinforcement: review phonics and segmenting words and suggest books that may be of interest.*

Another area to examine is the child's file.

Look for the results of an IQ test. Some boards give group IQ tests to all students at certain grades, such as Grade 3 or 4. You would find a statement of the child's intelligence, such as low average, average, high average, or superior. A child may also have had an individual IQ test, such as the Wechsler Scales of Intelligence (WISC), which would have been administered by a psychologist or psychometrist. There would be a full report indicating the child's areas of strengths and weaknesses, such as language, arithmetic, or visual-motor skills; his or her IQ; and suggestions for classroom accommodations, if required.

You may also find a copy of an IEP that, for whatever reason, is not being followed. This may sound surprising, but if a child has arrived at your school from a different board or even from a school within your own board, the file may not arrive until mid-October. If the child or parent has not informed you of an exceptionality and an IEP, you would not know that one existed unless you read the student's records.

As you go through the file, read the previous report cards and note the marks and teachers' comments. These records may support your own observations. Sometimes, the report cards offer no clue as to the present functioning of a student. In this case, trust your own observations and act upon them.

Next, read any other pertinent documents. These may include the results of an eye examination, hearing test, or group-administered achievement tests, such as the Canadian Test of Basic Skills (CTBS). In summary, read the file to find out about the past academic performance of the child and clues as to why the child is performing at his or her current level.

When making observations about academic performance, the important things to remember are to observe over time, to be as specific as possible, to note any clusters of strengths or weaknesses, and to verify them with previous records.

---

### Suggestions for Working with Parents

Be sure to speak with the parents of any child about whom you have concerns. You may gain valuable information about past performance and successful accommodations.

The keys to successful relationships with parents of children at risk or who have exceptionalities are *to understand their perspective and to communicate regularly with them*. With few exceptions, parents are motivated by love for and commitment to their children. They want what they feel is best for them. They also are the experts on their children. Although you have training and experience, your contact with students is episodic: you see a student for only 10 months or so. Parents, on the other hand, have a continuous relationship with their children.

Hence, they can provide you with insights about the child and how to work effectively with him. As well, they will often provide support for your work in the classroom.

Communicate your concerns about a student's progress to the parents. If this is your first contact with the parents, you must be empathetic, positive, and tactful. I recommend using the telephone for the initial contact with the parents. Before you make the call, gather your records and observational data so that you will have it close by you when you speak to them. Use the telephone at school instead of the one at your residence as most people have call display, and you may not want the student to know your home telephone number. *Always* begin the conversation with a positive comment about the student, such as "Your daughter appears to be doing well in math" or "Your son is able to express himself well during large-group discussions." Then state that you have noticed over the past few weeks some difficulties with oral reading, written expression, or submission of assignments. Describe your observations in a calm and confident voice. Use language that the parent can understand. If the difficulty is something that could be noticed at home or one that may have surfaced before, ask whether the parent is aware of the same thing. Then tell the parent how you plan to address the difficulty. At this point, the parent may offer some suggestions — do your best to incorporate them into your plan. If parents offer to work with their child at home, advise them about what could be done.

If the parent appears to be hostile or apathetic, or disagrees with your observations, do not press the point. Politely ask if you can work with the child and implement your plan. If the parent agrees, then you may put the accommodations into place. If the parent does not give permission, then put away your plan until the parent and the student are willing to work with you. Fortunately, this scenario does not happen often: most parents are grateful that a teacher is willing to assist their child in overcoming a difficulty at school.

Conclude your initial contact by making arrangements for future communication. Mutually acceptable means might include the student's agenda, weekly telephone calls, and e-mail.

### Junior high and high school students

Making detailed observations on each of your 120 students is difficult because you may not see each student every day. However, you may have noticed some whose academic performance is well above or below the standard or those who frequently exhibit very inappropriate behaviors.

The most important things to concentrate on are the student's marks, ability to hand in work on time, and attendance. Record keeping is obviously important here. You likely record the results of all tests, and after three tests you will begin to note the obvious patterns of achievement. In other words, you will notice whether a student has failed two or three of the three tests. You will also see which students have done very well on two or three of the three tests. If possible, note the areas in which a student may be having difficulty, for example, questions that require memorization, understanding of the passage, logical thought, or ability to express ideas in writing.

A second area in which to keep records is on whether the students are submitting assignments on time and if daily homework is completed. You might use a class list and check off each student's name when an assignment is submitted. As well, at the beginning of each class, have the students open their notebooks to show you their completed homework. Make note of those students who have completed or not completed it. You can follow this same record-keeping procedure for bringing equipment to class, such as shorts and t-shirts for physical education, geometry sets for math, and writing materials, textbooks, and notebooks for other classes.

The third area in which to keep records is attendance. Note all absences or late arrivals. If there are many, examine your records and note the day of the week and the day in the school's cycle. You may observe that the student is away every Friday or every Day Two in your school's cycle. If no pattern is apparent, then consider what was taught, done, or had to be submitted on the days of the absences. You may see a pattern of behaviors motivated by avoidance of a particular type of work, for example, oral presentations or written assignments. Also note the number of absences. Excessive absences may be linked to poor academic performance.

Another opportunity to make observations about your students is during the teaching of your lesson. Note who answers questions and who appears to understand the concepts. As well, when you circulate after giving the instruction, make the same notations about degree of understanding, speed of work completion, and attention span. Note, too, if a student avoids work by skipping class, talking to others, not bringing materials to class, requesting to sharpen a pencil or visit the washroom, or putting his or her head on the desk — these types of observations may be written in a private journal. Note the frequency of behaviors over time. A single occasion of incomplete homework or classroom chatter is not a behavior pattern; many observations of specific behaviors over two to four weeks will help you determine patterns.

After noting patterns of academic performance and classroom behaviors that may contribute to that performance, read the student's file. Note the marks in the subject area from past years and the teachers' comments. This information may support your own observations. Also read any psychological and medical reports in the student's file. A psychological report will provide information about a child's level of intelligence and areas of strength and weakness. You may also find an IEP that may or may not be in effect. A child may have an IEP that is supposed to be followed, but has not been read by the teachers. When a student changes schools, the files may arrive at the new school months after the classes have begun. As well, parents may have assumed that the school is aware of their child's needs and not inform the teachers. It also happens that when a student moves on to junior high or high school, an IEP may no longer be followed. The student's progress may be such that accommodations are no longer needed, a student may choose to do things without assistance, or a student may decide against taking part in the gifted program.

When you see a score in the student's records that looks like a decimal, here is how to interpret it. For example, a reading comprehension score of 5.6 means that the student is comprehending at the Grade 5, six month level.

Note any reports on hearing or vision. In junior high and high school, students may not want to wear their hearing aids or glasses, which can prove to be a hindrance to their academic performance. There may also be a report from a physician on attention span or Attention Deficit/Hyperactivity Disorder. Finally, the file may contain the results of standardized group achievement or ability testing, which could give clues to present academic performance. For example, if a student's reading comprehension and vocabulary are both 18 months below grade level, the student may have difficulty with tasks that require reading (e.g., multiple choice tests, instructions, and problem solving in math). Another example is a student whose verbal comments suggest high intelligence, but whose assignments and tests are of average quality. By reading the files, you may find that this student used to be in a gifted program; by talking with her, you may discover that she purposely gets average marks to fit in socially.

## Disruptive, Withdrawn, or Unusual Behaviors

You will readily notice those students who behave disruptively within the first two hours of the first day of school. Children who show signs of being withdrawn, however, may go undetected for several months as you concentrate on setting routines and dealing with the disruptive students. Do make note of avoidance behaviors, particularly in play or social situations, such as recess or group activities. Also make note of autistic-like behaviors (see Chapter 11) and the presence of physical or verbal tics, which may indicate Tourette syndrome (see Chapter 11).

There are two basic ways of recording behaviors: tally charts and anecdotal reports. When reviewing your observations over two to four weeks, note the frequency and intensity of the behaviors. Note any *patterns* of occurrence, for example, argumentation or avoidance behaviors right after certain tasks have been assigned. Whichever method of observation you choose, be discreet about collecting the data.

### Tally counts

Tally counts are a method of counting the number of times a behavior is observed. They involve making a vertical stroke every time you note a particular behavior. When you have four vertical strokes, the fifth one is a horizontal one through the other four. A tally count may be used to establish the frequency of such behaviors as wandering, pencil sharpening, calling out, going to the washroom, or any off-task behaviors.

A tally may be done for the entire day or for certain intervals or periods of the day. For example, an elementary teacher who notices that a child is out of his or her seat often may want to make observations of wandering over a three-day period. A teacher of the intermediate grades may want to use a tally sheet to note the number of times a student talks during the class period over a three-day time span. Or a teacher may want to use a tally count to observe off-task behaviors in five-minute intervals. In this instance, it's best if there is another adult in the class who can spend time observing a particular student.

Either method of tally counting will give you an idea as to whether the behaviors are excessive. Then from your observations, you can decide if the behaviors are interfering with the student's academic performance. You will also have baseline data with which to compare the behaviors after you have implemented your strategy for managing them.

### Anecdotal reports

This method of observing children involves making entries in a private journal. The short reports may be written in full sentences or in point-form notes. They are your personal means of noting details about specific behaviors, such as arguing, temper tantrums, or defiance.

When describing the incidents in which these behaviors occur, you may find it helpful to adopt the A B C method (**A**ntecedent, **B**ehavior, **C**onsequence).

First, note what happened before the negative behavior occurred, in other words, the *antecedent* action. For example, just before the disruption occurred, a task that the child did not want to do was assigned, group work was announced, or he or she spoke to another student. Note what happened just before the student became defiant or angry.

In one tally count, the teacher discovered that a child was out of his seat five times during a 40-minute period.

<del>+++/</del>

Next, note the *exact* behaviors, such as the words the student used to challenge your authority, the nature of the fight that broke out between two students, the gist of the argument between you and the student, or the actions observed during a temper tantrum.

The final observations to record are the consequences of the behaviors or how the incident was resolved. A student who swore at you would have been sent to the office, as would the two students who were fighting. A student in the midst of a temper tantrum may have abruptly begun to cry. A student who was arguing with you about the senselessness of an assignment may have stormed out of the room. The behaviors immediately after the disruption are also recorded under Consequences. You may also record how the incident was resolved, for example, with an apology, a suspension from school, or a return to work.

Reviewing your anecdotal records on a student over a two- to four-week period will give you some ideas as to behavior patterns. For example, you may notice that a child may avoid unpleasant tasks by putting her head on a desk, wandering, or defying your authority. The third type of behavior may land the child in the principal's office, where the work could be successfully avoided. When making anecdotal reports, again, be discreet, and place the journal in a locked file cabinet when you are not making entries. As well, the more richly described the incident, the easier it will be to note patterns of behavior.

## Cautionary Notes About Making Observations of Students

### Keep developmental stages in mind

When reviewing your observational data, ask yourself the question if what you are seeing is within the broad range of normal behavior for the child's age group. For younger children, consider whether the lower academic performance or behavior problem is due to a short-term developmental lag. In other words, the child does not have a developmental disability or a learning disability, but is simply not as ready to learn or as mature as the others in the class. This may be true of some of the children born in the fall of the year, assuming that the enrolment cut-off date is December 31.

Some academic problems and behaviors may be explained as a developmental lag up until Grade 5 or 6. For example, some children may struggle with reading until the end of Grade 2, but suddenly catch on in Grade 3. Other children may be able to think abstractly at age 10, while others may need a lot of concrete materials to learn concepts until age 14. Therefore, remember to consider the normal stages of development when reviewing your observational data and note those areas that seem to be outside the normal range. If you need to refresh your memory on developmental stages, consult any textbook in child psychology or educational psychology. You may also ask the special education teacher at your school about specific students.

### Consider whose problem this is

For disruptive or unusual behaviors, always ask yourself "Is this beyond the normal range for a child of that age *or* is it that I am intolerant or haven't planned this lesson properly?"

Every teacher has different tolerance levels for certain behaviors. For example, some teachers permit more talking and movement in a classroom than others. It must also be noted that some children require more opportunities to talk and move than others. Sometimes, teachers blame the child when they should be examining their own tolerance levels and ways of conducting their lessons. Ask yourself how much talking or wandering do you expect to see in a given activity. If you are having the students work in groups or at centres, then there will be more talking and moving than if you are conducting a teacher-centred lesson. Also ask yourself how much talking and moving you can tolerate. You may find that you will reassess the amount of talking and wandering you will permit in the classroom.

One of the most important acts of teaching is to plan your lessons carefully. Aim to have all the materials prepared ahead of time and in place for use by yourself and the students. Try to plan lessons that involve the children as much as possible, incorporate a multisensory approach, and include opportunities or activities for children who need reinforcement and enrichment. There should be no "dead" spots in the lesson which tempt the students to exhibit off-task behaviors. Through thorough planning, you will find that you're better organized and deliver the lesson more effectively, which allows the students to learn more in your class.

### Learn all you can about students who have identified exceptionalities

The previous comments have related to *unidentified* students who are at risk or who may have a gift. However, if you have a student who has been identified as having a specific exceptionality, read the child's file and, in particular, the IEP, which will state among other things the accommodations that are required by a student, and supporting documents, such as a physician's report or the psychological report. Beyond that, read as much as you can to gain a *general* idea of the exceptionality. Talk to the parents and the child about specific needs. For example, a child with a hearing impairment may require the use of an FM system and as much print information as possible. Or a child with low vision may require more or less light as the day goes on to accommodate levels of eye strain. As well, talk to the child's previous teachers to find out what techniques were used successfully with the child. Finally, make your *own* observations in the context of other information. For example, a report on a student with Down syndrome may state that during testing the child was able to do only certain things; however, you may find that in a more relaxed situation the student can perform much more than what was reported.

## Referring Students for Testing

After making your observations, you may find that your hunches about a possible problem in academic performance, disruptive behavior, or potential giftedness were justified. You may want to refer the child for testing.

First, discuss your findings with the principal, vice-principal, head of special education, guidance counselor, or any other designated person. Review your data with this person or team in order to determine whether the child should be referred for testing. You might decide in favor of an immediate referral for testing or that you introduce some accommodations or behavior management programs *before* the child is referred. Given that it takes so long for testing to occur, the latter course of action is usually taken.

If it is decided that testing is desirable, discuss your observations with the child's parents. It should be noted that the conversation about testing would *not* have been the first held with the parents. After collecting your data about a child's academic performance, you would have informed the parents by telephone or at a meeting at the school.

When testing is recommended, most schools want to meet with the parents to review the observational data and any initial achievement testing or screening done by the special education teacher. At the meeting, the parents may state that they have similar concerns and may approve the testing. However, the parents may not want the child to undergo any tests at this time. Each district has different rules about parental approval for testing, and it is important that you know whether any formalized testing may occur without parental consent.

If you and your colleagues decide that you should implement an *informal plan* to address the student's needs, then describe your observations to the parents and explain how you intend to accommodate the child's needs. Whenever you speak to parents, have all of your data with you so that you can state specific marks on specific tests given on specific dates, or the precise dates that the child was absent from your third period class, or the exact inappropriate behaviors that were shown in which situation on a specific date.

Be prepared for a negative reaction, at least initially. No parent likes to hear that there is a problem with their child. *Listen* to what the parents have to say about the child. Ask if the parents have noticed any difficulties or specific behaviors at home. Let the parents know what you are going to try and tell them that you will call again in a week to provide an update. Since a parent may want to meet with you to discuss the plan in person, you should be open to this suggestion.

Bear in mind two important points: if you raise a problem about a child with a parent, then you have to address it — *never* call a parent just to complain — and be sure to inform the parents of the progress of the child as your informal plan is being implemented. In this way the parents will know that before testing was recommended, the school tried to address their child's problems.

Whether the child is slated for testing or not, you will have to develop a plan for working with the child in the classroom. As soon as the child is suspected of having a disability or a behavior problem, or as requiring enrichment, you have a moral obligation to adapt your teaching strategies and possibly modify the curriculum to meet that child's needs. However, as you will discover, meeting the needs of these students is not burdensome. More often than not it involves making some minor adjustments to your teaching behaviors and possibly some modifications to your lessons and units. And remember: By making observations, you have already begun the process of working successfully with that student.

# CHAPTER 2

# Formulating Goals

After making observations of a student and deciding that some action is needed, think about targeting specific areas to address the child's strengths or weaknesses. List the student's strengths and weaknesses. For the weaknesses, include any observational data you may have, for example, the number of times out of his seat, her reading levels, and the number of absences. Writing this information may help you prioritize the weaknesses or strengths, beginning with the ones that require immediate attention to those that can wait.

Should you make a plan for every student? No. Just develop informal plans for those who have not been through a formal identification process and who seem to have a number of strengths or weaknesses that you, as the classroom teacher, can address.

The next step is to select the top two or three areas and develop them into your goals to address the needs of the student. As you address these goals, introduce the next ones on your priority list. You may do these two activities on your own or with the resource/special education teacher at your school. I recommend identifying strengths and weaknesses and developing goals before talking with the parents. In this way you can present them at the initial meeting and make revisions based on the input of the student and parents.

Three examples of observational data translated into goals are presented. The students whose cases are presented are composites of children with whom I have worked in elementary, junior high, and high schools. I have personally used or seen used all of the strategies suggested for each child. I know they all work.

## The Real Problem

ANDREW

Andrew was a Grade 9 student who was initially viewed as having a behavior problem. At the meeting of the Grade 9 teachers with guidance and resource personnel at the end of September, the vice-principal noted that within the first month of school Andrew had skipped two classes (both in English and on days when written assignments were to be submitted). The English teacher added that on four occasions Andrew had arrived late for her class. The vice-principal then made a comment about this boy "heading towards a year of office detentions." Andrew was thus "flagged."

The English teacher's thoughts turned to the weaknesses she had observed in Andrew's written work. She wondered aloud if Andrew was practising avoidance behaviors to get out of doing the written work required in English.

*Weaknesses/Priority*
– arrives late (4) and skips classes
  (up to 10) (ongoing)
– easily off-task (ongoing)
– refuses to complete some
  assignments or portions of some
  assignments (ongoing)
– hands in assignments late (7/9 were
  late)
– doesn't always bring his notebook
  and pen to class (6 times in 6
  weeks) (ongoing)
– written assignments too short (1)
– handwriting very messy (2)

*Strengths*
– participates in oral discussions
– is able to express his ideas well
  orally

*Goals*
1. To lengthen written responses
2. To improve neatness of written
   work

Over the next two weeks, she collected data on Andrew's strengths and
weaknesses. The results are shown in the margin.

The English teacher discussed her observations with Andrew privately. He
stated that he disliked writing because he found it difficult to organize his
thoughts and that he was embarrassed to hand in his work due to his poor
handwriting.

The teacher decided that the most important goal at this time was to lengthen
Andrew's written responses to test questions and the assignments that he
submitted. Andrew's marks in English were below average, and she felt that if
he learned how to organize his thoughts on paper, his grades would improve.
She also believed that if Andrew experienced some success in her class, he
would be more motivated to arrive on time and not to skip.

The teacher's second goal for Andrew was to see the neatness of his written
assignments improve. Andrew's handwriting was difficult to read; the letters
were crowded and poorly formed. He also wrote slowly. The teacher felt that if
Andrew could submit more legible assignments, then he might be more willing
to hand them in.

Finally, the teacher wanted to ensure that Andrew experienced more success
in her course generally: she wanted to give him opportunities to use his oral
strengths. She had a hunch that many of the avoidance behaviors he practised
were due to a feeling of being unsuccessful in English. It was now almost the
middle of the semester, and the progress reports would soon be issued. Since
Andrew's achievement mark in English was only in the 50 percent range, the
teacher felt that this would be an opportune time to discuss the goals with him.
She knew that the necessity for doing this would not be warmly received by his
professional parents.

The teacher was able to look beyond Andrew's behavior to see the real
problem: written work. She realized that Andrew's "behaviors" were a means of
avoiding the activities in which he was unsuccessful. The teacher felt that by
addressing Andrew's weaknesses, the symptoms of a behavior problem would
decrease.

In our next case study we will see how an elementary teacher handled another
"behavior" problem.

## The Reason Behind the Behavior

ALEX

It was mid-November, and the Grade 5 teacher was at her wit's end with Alex's
behaviors. Alex seemed to be even more active in the classroom than earlier in
the fall. The girl left her seat many times during the day, constantly jiggled her
right leg, and talked constantly. Her attention span seemed to be shorter than
that of the other children, and she blurted out answers constantly.

Alex's behaviors were now at a level that the teacher was finding intolerable.
Her constant talking and wandering were disrupting the other students in the
class. The teacher had tried nagging, threatening, and raising her voice
occasionally, but none of these techniques were working. To make matters
worse, Alex was beginning to argue with the teacher, who now felt quite
frustrated. The teacher wanted to ensure a reasonable learning environment for
all the students, but Alex's actions were disrupting it. As well, she didn't
appreciate this student's threats to her own power in the classroom.

After one exhausting day with Alex, the teacher sat at her desk and asked herself if it was Alex's problem — or hers. Was she becoming less tolerant of Alex's behaviors, or were the behaviors increasing to such a level that no one could tolerate them? In short, whose problem was this?

After thinking about Alex's behaviors in September and October, the teacher determined that the impulsivity and restlessness had increased. The other students were now complaining about Alex's excessive talking and about being bothered when she was out of her seat. The teacher also acknowledged that her own tolerance might be declining as the term progressed.

As she examined a list of characteristics of children with AD/HD (similar to the one printed in Chapter 6), the teacher wondered if Alex had suddenly developed AD/HD. She put aside that idea, however, as she doubted that the symptoms had persisted for at least six months. She then thought that maybe she should try to see the good parts of Alex, that maybe she was focusing too closely on the irritating behaviors. The teacher did think of two positive characteristics. Alex was a good athlete and a member of a swimming team, and her creative writing showed that she had a vivid imagination.

The teacher then wondered if something at home was causing Alex anxiety because some children react to stress by behaving in the ways Alex was. She decided to check Alex's file to see if comments about this type of behavior had appeared on previous report cards and to talk to Alex's parents.

The teacher read Alex's file, whose comments suggested that the girl had previously had problems "focusing." Many youngsters have short attention spans, however. She did notice that in Grade 1, Alex's teacher had commented about aggressive behavior in the final term. The teacher also observed that Alex's marks were well above average on all report cards.

Before she contacted Alex's mother, the teacher decided to do some tally counts and anecdotal reports about her behavior. Over a three-day period she noted the following:

- Alex was out of her seat between 15 and 17 times a day.
- She talked constantly while doing her seatwork.
- She blurted out answers during the instructional part of any lesson between four and seven times.
- An argument occurred over the completion of a creative writing assignment.

In the latter instance, it was obvious that Alex didn't want to write an alternate ending to the story they had just read in language arts. She stated that she didn't know what to write and argued. The teacher raised her voice, and Alex continued arguing. The teacher then threatened to send her into the hall to write her story, and Alex still argued. The teacher moved Alex's desk into the hall, and Alex wrote nothing. The teacher was surprised that Alex didn't want to do the creative writing, because her stories were always well done. She was also surprised at how quickly the argument escalated and how readily she used threats when she felt she had lost control over Alex.

The teacher telephoned Alex's mother and discussed the changes in the girl's behavior. She wondered if any changes at home might have affected Alex's behaviors. Alex's mother responded that her husband had just been diagnosed with a heart problem and was now on a waiting list for treatment. In the last few weeks, there had been much tension in the house over the husband's medical condition. She also said that she, too, had noticed that Alex was behaving more aggressively, particularly towards her younger brother, and that Alex was arguing more with her over the bedtime hour and about making her bed. She said that at the most recent swimming practice Alex had sat alone on the deck instead of swimming in the pool. The mother assumed that Alex had misbehaved, but did not pursue it. She wondered if anything could be done to help Alex in school. The teacher told her that she would talk to the special education teacher and get back to her.

The next afternoon Alex's teacher and the special education teacher met and reviewed observational data that had been collected. They also discussed Alex's strengths and possible behavioral goals for her.

Alex's teacher prioritized the two behaviors that the other students found disruptive to their own learning, that is, the wandering and the talking. She knew that she couldn't eliminate these behaviors, but they had to decrease in order to be tolerable to others. The teacher also felt that the arguing had to stop as this set a bad example for the rest of the class. Finally, she thought that if she made some adjustments in her teaching style, Alex's shorter attention span and habit of blurting out answers might be manageable in the classroom.

In the two previous cases, we have seen teachers looking beyond negative behaviors and examining the strengths of the student, as well as their own teaching styles. I have found that how I act affects the way a student acts. It seems so obvious, but sometimes we are so "stuck" in our ways that we automatically blame the student when we could act to improve the child's behaviors. Keep in mind that you will not likely be able to eliminate all of a student's inappropriate behaviors, but you can usually make them tolerable.

In the last case presented here, we meet Erik, who shows no behavior problems.

*Weaknesses/Priority*
– out of seat 15–17 times per day (1)
– talks constantly (2)
– blurts out answers 4–7 times per day (ongoing)
– short attention span (ongoing)
– argues (3)

*Strengths*
– athletic; is on a swim team
– vivid imagination; writes well

*Goals*
1. To decrease the out-of-seat behaviors
2. To decrease the talking
3. To decrease the arguing

## Recognition of Gifts

ERIK

Erik was a Grade 7 student attending the intermediate program that was housed in a high school. Erik's father was in the military, and the family had moved three times in the last six years. They had just settled in the area this past August and believed that this move would be the last.

At a meeting of the Grade 7 and 8 teachers at the end of September, the boy's homeroom teacher expressed delight in teaching such a capable student. He had noticed that Erik had some strong abilities in math and computers. The music teacher then stated that he too had noticed that Erik was doing very well in music. (At this school every student had to learn how to play an instrument, and Erik had chosen the saxophone.) However, the other teachers commented that Erik was a quiet boy who was performing in the average to above average range. The special education teacher was perusing the file and noted that there was no record of any ability testing, likely because Erik had missed scheduled group tests during his frequent moves.

The homeroom and music teachers spoke privately to Erik about their observations and recommended that he participate in enrichment activities in the areas of English and music. They explained that they would develop the ideas and have a meeting with him and his parents within the next two weeks. Erik responded favorably. He explained that he was bored in school and was happy that the teachers had finally noticed his abilities. He agreed to consider the enrichment activities as long as he had a say in them and that his work wouldn't be obvious to his peers. He was trying to fit in and didn't want to be ostracized before he had a chance to make a few friends.

## Taking the Initiative

The teachers of the students described noticed that the children's academic performance or behaviors were beyond the broad range of what they considered to be normal.

For Andrew and Alex, the teachers took time to collect data to check out their hunches. Specifically, they wanted to have an accurate "read" on disruptive and avoidance types of behaviors. With these data in hand, they were able to verify their hunches. However, note that these teachers collected data not only on weaknesses, but also on strengths. Too often we focus on weaknesses and ignore the positive things that are happening for a child. As well, as you will see later, strengths may be used to address weaknesses.

For Erik, whose teachers thought he had some gifts, specific data were not collected. Instead, his effort and achievement in specific subject areas were noted. The teachers decided that they wanted to provide enrichment opportunities; as there was no IEP, the student was free to participate or not.

Goal setting based on observations applies to teachers, as well. In the case of Alex, who was displaying disruptive behaviors, the teacher examined not only Alex's weaknesses, but her own. After much thought, the teacher realized that she could improve her curriculum planning, teaching techniques, class management, and discipline. She reflected that if she changed the environment, then Alex's behaviors might be more tolerable for everyone.

The three teachers described above showed a willingness to act on observations made about their students. It took courage to make changes in their programs and teaching approaches that would benefit these students and others in the class. These caring teachers demonstrated that they were committed to doing the best job possible for all of their students.

# CHAPTER 3

# Developing Adaptations

Once you have formulated general goals to address a student's needs, that is, either remediation or enrichment, it's time to consider the range of possible adaptations.

Discussing your observations with the special education teacher is always wise because you will gain some ideas on what accommodations would be appropriate. In many schools, the special education teacher or resource teacher works with small groups of students, but also acts as an in-school consultant for teachers, providing them with ideas about classroom accommodations. Once you know possible ways to provide remediation or enrichment, then you can begin to decide which ones will work in your classroom with a particular child.

Both an IEP and an informal plan list strengths, weaknesses, and accommodations that are developed by teachers, parents, and students. Both guide the teacher when making accommodations for a student. However, the IEP is a legal document based on the results of standardized testing; an informal plan is based on the teacher's systematic observations.

After developing possible adaptations for each goal, write an informal plan. (See Chapter 4 for examples and the planning sheet in the Appendices.) Then, meet with the child, the parents, the special education teacher, and the principal to discuss your observations, goals, and plan to address the needs. The meeting should occur as soon as your informal plan is written and at a time that is convenient for everyone. It will allow you to present your observations and proposed accommodations. It also provides an opportunity for others to react to your ideas and to have input into the informal plan. During your discussion, new information may be presented or other ideas for accommodations suggested and added to the plan.

Next, decide on a time frame in which to implement the adaptations: one school term is usually long enough for any improvements in academic performance or behavior to be sustained. By the end of the time period, you may safely conclude that work habits or reading scores have improved, or that enrichment work has been appropriate.

The next step is to implement the teaching techniques and curriculum adaptations you have planned.

Always respect the wishes of parents and students.

Most parents will support your ideas to address the needs of their child. However, parents may not feel that any accommodations are necessary and likely would have told you this during your telephone calls before the meeting. In this case, respect their wishes, but file the observations and plan in a secure spot. As well, you may be in a situation where the student refuses to participate in such things as self-monitoring of behavior, a reward system, or enrichment activities. In this instance, it's best to identify what the student is willing to do and begin with this. If the student refuses to participate in the entire plan, you can do little else but explain the possible consequences of receiving no assistance and acknowledge that participation is voluntary. However, file your plan in a secure place and be open to the possibility of implementing it when the student is ready to work with you.

## Introduction of Coping Strategies

ANDREW

Andrew's English teacher, who had taken a course in special education, thought that this Grade 9 student might have a mild learning disability in the area of written expression. She believed that his attempt to hide his weakness was turning into a behavior problem.

To avoid drawing hasty conclusions that may be incorrect, collect your data systematically, compare them with the information you have on learning disabilities, and talk to the special education teacher.

After the meeting of the Grade 9 teachers, the teacher talked to the head of the special education department about her observations, goals for Andrew, and possible accommodations. In response, the special education teacher showed her a list of learning disability characteristics. Andrew seemed to be showing some of them in the area of written expression. However, perhaps he had just never learned how to organize his thoughts before writing. As well, the English teacher couldn't say that this problem had persisted over several months. What she did know was that by the time any testing results would be available, the semester would be over, and Andrew would no longer be in her class.

The English teacher decided that a plan was needed *now* to help Andrew during the second half of the semester. She sought to give him opportunities to use his oral skills and to provide coping skills to help him improve his written work in English and other subject areas. She wanted to give Andrew more opportunities to succeed. She believed that if he were successful, then he would come to class with his notebook and pen and remain on-task. The English teacher also wanted to use Andrew's strength in oral communication whenever possible. Finally, she decided on adaptations that were appropriate for the *entire* class so that Andrew wouldn't feel uncomfortable.

As a teacher, be very careful about diagnosing a student as having a disability or AD/HD without proper assessment by a psychologist or physician. You may have a hunch about a student, but it is important to examine *all* possible causes of low academic performance and negative behaviors.

In mid-October the teacher met with Andrew, his parents, the head of the special education department, and the vice-principal. She described what she had done thus far and sought their input. Andrew's parents were surprised that a high school teacher had taken the time to work with their son. They admitted that Andrew was a "master" of avoidance behaviors and that since Grade 6 some weakness in written work had been detected, but not seriously addressed. They also confirmed that Andrew would rather talk than write, if given the choice, and they gave their consent to have their son tested for a possible learning disability. They expressed their disappointment in Andrew's attendance record, but were happy to be informed of it.

Andrew was quiet throughout most of the meeting; however, he did agree to cooperate with the English teacher and try her accommodations. He was feeling desperate as his parents knew about the skipping and the low mark in English. He felt as though he had to make some effort to turn things around. The next meeting was scheduled for February after the first semester.

The accommodations that Andrew's teacher developed to help him are outlined on the next page.

## Written assignments

For pieces in which Andrew had to state and argue a point of view, the teacher adopted the following practice.

---

**Writing from a Point of View**

1. Discuss with the entire class possible points of view they could take in a brief, five-paragraph essay and write key words on the board.
2. Give students a copy of Frame for Writing a Five-Paragraph Essay (see page 121) which they can use to organize their ideas into major and supporting points. Each grouping of a major point and supporting ones would become a separate paragraph.
3. Ask students to rank their points from 1 to 3, with 1 being the strongest and 3 the weakest.
4. Direct students to write the introduction, then a paragraph with point #2, then one with #3 (the weakest in the middle), one with point #1 to send a strong message, and the conclusion.

---

Discussing the answers to questions with the student allows him to show that he knows the material, even though his written work may not reflect it. The struggling English student will also feel more confident that he has the correct answers and may volunteer answers during discussions.

Typed copies usually look neater and motivate students to write more than they would if hand-writing an assignment. Typewritten text takes up less space than handwritten text, and students feel that more ideas are needed to add length.

Even though Andrew had not had a formal assessment, the special education teacher arranged for him to write in the resource room if he needed more time. You could set up a similar accommodation for a student who writes very slowly.

As much as possible, let students use their strengths. Oral communication was Andrew's.

It's desirable for students to monitor their own behaviors. They then have something to base a change upon.

In support of this model, the teacher provided samples of completed assignments to illustrate how to organize the material or points. She also worked with Andrew in formulating his points.

The teacher decided upon the following ways to accommodate the student:

✔ Discuss with Andrew privately the answers to questions related to the study of novels, short stories, or plays.
✔ Talk to Andrew about the need for more time to complete written assignments. If an extension is required, then he must request it before the assignment is due and the due date must be mutually agreed upon.
✔ Occasionally permit assignments to be done orally.

## Handwriting

✔ When Andrew writes by hand, encourage him to use every second line and to space out the letters of the words so that they may be read.
✔ Inform all students as to when the school's computer lab is open for use. Encourage Andrew to type his assignments.

## General accommodations

✔ For tests and examinations, try to arrange the following: that Andrew have up to one-third more time to write them; that he write as much as he can for each answer and then tells an adult what he wanted to write (the adult will write the sections of the oral answer that did not appear in written form); and that Andrew be permitted to write answers to test and examination questions in point form.
✔ Encourage Andrew to take part in large- and small-group discussions. Structure small-group work so that Andrew does not serve as the recorder.
✔ Set up a chart with Andrew whereby he records how often he arrives on time, brings his notebook and pen, and submits assignments; however, continue to record late arrivals, absences, and late or non-submissions. Praise Andrew discreetly for coming to class and submitting assignments.

A bus pass or shoe works well as collateral. The student won't get too far without either!

Students need to know that teachers are working to help them, not just out to catch their mistakes.

✔ If required, have looseleaf paper available for Andrew to use; also, be prepared to lend him a pen in exchange for collateral for the length of a class period.

✔ Try to develop a rapport with Andrew and other students before the class begins by talking about topics in which *they* are interested, such as sports, music, or events at the school. I have always found that just greeting the students as they walk in the classroom with a smile or a simple "hi" is an effective way to open the door to a possible conversation.

✔ When marking a student's assignments, provide as much feedback as possible through written comments in the margin.

We saw that Andrew was noticed by his teachers due to the poor quality of his written work and his passive avoidance behaviors. Alex, on the other hand, presents a very different case. Her academic work is at grade level, but her aggressive and non-compliant behaviors are disturbing the entire class.

## Ways to Address Disruptive Behavior

ALEX Alex's teacher had discussed goals for Alex with the special education teacher, and they later met to develop some ways of addressing the Grade 5 student's disruptive behaviors. The following are the techniques that the classroom teacher adopted.

### Wandering

✔ Plan some lessons that enable Alex to move around. Using manipulatives and organizing learning centres should do this.

✔ Use task analysis to break an assignment into smaller pieces. As Alex completes each section, praise her, and permit her to go for a drink of water. Remind her that when she goes for her drink, she has to be back within one minute, and she is not allowed to touch others or talk to them.

Once students become aware of how often they behave in a certain way, they may be motivated to reduce it.

✔ Have Alex monitor her own behavior by keeping a daily tally count of her wandering. The tally count would be divided into four sections to correspond to the four time blocks of the day. Keep an independent tally count to compare numbers with Alex.

✔ Establish a number of times per day that Alex could be out of her seat and reward her each day with a sticker in her planner if she stays within that limit.

✔ Reteach the rules on moving about the room and not bothering others to the entire class. Be prepared to remind Alex of these rules whenever required.

### Talking

Providing a student with two desks works when the classroom is large enough to place a desk away from other students.

✔ Assign Alex one desk at the front of the room and a second one at the back. Have Alex come to the front for the instruction part of the lesson and complete her seatwork at the desk at the back. If necessary, turn the desk to the wall so that her voice will not carry.

✔ Plan more lessons involving groups. The talking wouldn't be as disruptive and might even be focused on the task.

**Arguing**

✔ Provide more choices in classroom work, such as in creative writing, so that Alex can find something that interests her. When she doesn't want to do an assignment, give her the choice of doing it now or for homework.

✔ Use the broken record technique in response to her arguing about not doing work.

✔ Enforce the "hands up" rule when the children are answering questions and call on Alex as soon as she raises her hand. Use nonverbal cues to remind Alex to raise her hand or return to her seat.

✔ Plan interesting lessons featuring a variety of activities (e.g., teacher-directed, small-group work, and individual work). Also, consider planning a shorter instructional part to the lesson, if necessary.

✔ Use a multisensory method of teaching that incorporates visual, auditory, and tactile stimulation. (See page 56 for an example of how it may be used when teaching spelling.)

✔ Use I-messages in a quiet and calm voice when Alex does not follow the rules.

✔ Monitor Alex's behavior in the classroom as much as possible.

✔ Provide as much individual assistance as possible.

✔ Give Alex opportunities to "shine," for example, in physical education ask her to demonstrate certain skills that she can perform well.

✔ Develop a rapport with Alex by discussing her swimming and other interests.

For example, say, "In our class we do our work." Repeat this sentence in a calm, firm voice, moving close to the student and looking her in the eye. For most students, the arguing stops after three repetitions.

If the activity in the lesson changed about every 10 minutes, Alex's attention might be more focused than if she were just listening to the teacher talk.

An example of an I-message: The teacher could say, "I am disturbed when you are out of your seat because you are not completing your own work. I want you to stay at your desk and work on this assignment."

The overall strategy was to bring more structure to the classroom and to monitor Alex's behaviors more closely. However, at the same time the teacher realized that she had to "give" a little too. She had to make shorter presentations and provide more built-in activity, behave more calmly in the classroom, and recognize Alex's strengths whenever possible. She needed to alter the classroom environment so that she and Alex could both thrive.

Alex, her parents, the special education teacher, and the principal held a meeting to discuss the observations, goals, and the plan of action. As soon as the teacher finished speaking about the goals, Alex burst into tears and said that she didn't want her daddy to die. Her father quickly gathered her into his arms and explained that his medical condition was treatable, that he wasn't going to die. The adults realized that Alex had been very anxious about her father's health, which likely had been responsible for the sudden increase of disruptive behaviors. After Alex calmed down, the teacher explained the plan, and Alex agreed to try it. She said that she knew she had been "bad," but couldn't help the way she was acting these days. She said that the teacher's ideas might help her get back to "normal." The group decided to meet at the end of March, and over the next three months the plan would be implemented.

The stories of Andrew and Alex show how you can develop an informal plan to address the needs of students with academic and behavioral difficulties. The next case focuses on providing enrichment to a junior high school student who possessed some obvious gifts.

# Encouragement for Enrichment

ERIK

At an end-of-September meeting of Grade 7 and 8 teachers, Erik's homeroom teacher stated that he was very impressed by Erik's abilities in math and computers, while the music teacher wanted to allow Erik to advance his talent in playing the saxophone. Both teachers wanted to recognize Erik's strengths in a way that would make him feel comfortable in developing them. They were both concerned that if Erik remained unchallenged, he might not develop good work habits and could become disruptive in class. The teachers also noticed that Erik was shy and thought that participating in smaller groups devoted to areas in which he had abilities would make it easier for him to socialize.

The next week the homeroom and music teachers met with the special education teacher to brainstorm possible enrichment opportunities. The parents, Erik, the special education teacher, and the vice-principal were later invited to attend a meeting to discuss the teachers' observations and ideas for enrichment. After speaking with the parents and the administration, it was decided that Erik would not be tested. No gifted classes or enrichment programs were available at the school, and Erik's abilities in other subject areas were only above average. Moreover, Erik made it clear that he was willing to engage only in informal enrichment activities in math, computers, and music. Several options, outlined below, were identified.

Many students, like Erik, have gifts, but that alone does not make them candidates for IQ testing which measures ability in language and logical thinking. In Erik's case, he had abilities in logical thinking, but his language scores were not in the superior range. Moreover, he was not interested in attending a special program. Therefore testing was not considered.

> It is not unusual for a student who is bored to amuse himself by talking or disturbing others. Two things are important: look beyond the disruptive behavior to see if the child is bored and, if so, plan enrichment activities for him. When a child is interested in the work, he will be engaged in the tasks and will not disturb others.

> The word "encourage" is key to working with adolescents. You can acknowledge their abilities and talk to them about how they might enjoy participating in a competition, club, or team. You can also provide them with information about the activities. However, teenagers need to *choose* their own activities; your job is to recognize needs and provide opportunities for advancement.

## Math/Computers

- ✔ Encourage Erik to join the Engineering Club whose members enter the math and engineering contests and solve computer problems.
- ✔ Encourage Erik to enter the school's science fair, where winners go on to compete in provincial and national contests.
- ✔ Encourage Erik to do at least one extra project in computers by the end of the term. Use the Project Form to structure and record discussions on topics, process of collecting data, final product, and evaluation. Allow all of the students the opportunity to do this kind of work and earn extra marks so that Erik would not feel as though he were being singled out.
- ✔ During class time, ask open-ended questions that stimulate higher order thinking, include a problem of the day in math at the beginning of the period, and provide enrichment questions in both math and computers for Erik and other students who finish their work ahead of the others.

## Music

- ✔ Encourage Erik to join the Grade 7 Band.
- ✔ Encourage Erik to go through the Grade 7 music book at his own rate. Offer individual tutoring about the theory and technique as required. Give Erik sheet music of more challenging pieces that could be practised at home.
- ✔ Informally acknowledge him as the first saxophonist for the Grade 7 Band and find pieces for that band where the saxophone is featured.

✔ Later in the year, encourage Erik to join the Jazz Band for Grade 8 and promising Grade 7 students.

✔ Speak to Erik's parents about the possibility of private lessons.

## Responding Appropriately to Student Needs

In this chapter you have seen teachers working with others in developing adaptations to their own teaching style and the curriculum that they felt would provide the accommodations necessary for a student to succeed. In each case, the special education teacher was consulted for ideas on possible modifications. (You will find many modifications identified in Part B of this book.) The teachers also worked with other school personnel, the parents, and the student in developing an informal plan of action.

What teachers do depends on their students' needs.

The student's age is one factor to consider. For example, to address an academic weakness in a child in the primary or junior division, the teacher would normally develop a strategy focused on remediating the area of weakness. For someone such as Andrew, the strategy would be to teach coping skills to help the student perform better now and in the future. Providing *remediation* helps allow elementary students to gain the skills; teaching *coping skills*, such as using a calculator or spell check, helps enable older students to perform well to obtain the highest possible marks. If a student has previously had remediation work, then more of the same is unlikely to be helpful.

Student interests also need to be taken into account. Erik had a few specific gifts, so the strategy was to present as many opportunities for *enrichment* as possible and to allow him to engage in those of interest.

Alex was in a different situation. Her needs were not in the academic area at all; they related to emotional stress. In her case, the teacher worked with Alex and her parents to change the disruptive behaviors that signalled her worry about her father.

These stories confirm how caring and committed teachers can help their students improve and extend their performance.

# CHAPTER 4

# Implementing and Reviewing the Action Plan

*Wandering*

*Before*

$+\!+\!+\!+$

*After*

/

The final stage in the process of working with any student who needs remediation or enrichment is to discuss the student's progress since implementing the plan of action and make decisions about future directions.

When assessing a child's progress, it is helpful to use the same methods as were used during the observation phase a few weeks or months ago. For example, if you used informal teacher-made tests or tally counts when you began observing the child, use these methods again when you want to assess the child's progress since implementing the plan. In this way, you can make fairly valid comparisons of pre- and post-implementation behaviors and achievement. The tally counts at the left show the number of times a student wandered in a 30-minute period, before and after a plan was implemented.

After collecting this second set of data within a predetermined amount of time, arrange to meet with the parents, the child, the special education teacher, the principal (or designate), and any other involved people to make decisions about future adaptations. Present the initial data, provide a brief statement of the goals, describe the adaptations that were implemented, and summarize the final set of observational data. It should be noted that the results of psychological testing may or may not be available at the time of your second meeting. If these results are available, they will tell you about the student's total IQ score and the areas of strength and weakness. The psychologist who wrote the report will also note any learning disability or academic giftedness. Once everyone has had a chance to discuss the adaptations and outcomes, then the group can make decisions about continuing parts of the informal plan, making modifications to it, or incorporating it into the IEP that will be written later. The decisions will vary. In some cases, it may be decided that testing would be inappropriate, that a specific goal has been achieved, or that work should continue in specific areas.

As you read more about Andrew, Alex, and Erik, you will see how each of the students progressed with the accommodations and understand the rationale for the decisions that were made for each of them.

# Steps Towards Success

Between mid-October and the end of January, the English teacher let all of her students choose how they could best present some assignments: in writing, orally, or with a video. Andrew, whose strength was oral communication, gave oral presentations whenever possible. He also began participating more often in large-group discussions and small-group work. For the five-paragraph papers in which he expressed his views, Andrew followed the writing guide. He found that when his ideas were organized in point form on paper, writing them was easier. His ideas were better organized, but still not fully expressed.

The teacher initiated other ways of supporting students such as Andrew. She told the class that she would grant extensions, but only if they were requested before the due date. The maximum length was three days. Andrew now felt safe to ask for an extension, but needed only one between mid-October and January. When taking tests for English, he wrote his answers in point form, which helped him to complete the questions within the allotted time. For the first semester examinations, he was able to obtain extra time for English and wrote in the resource room; he didn't need extra time for his other subjects. Essentially, he sought ways to cope with his weakness in written expression by doing oral presentations, answering questions in point form, and taking extra time when full sentences were required.

> Resolving one problem, in this case, legibility, can lead to the discovery of another. For Andrew, it was spelling.

When Andrew began writing on every second line and spacing his letters so that the teacher could read his work, she discovered that Andrew had a spelling problem. He admitted that he was not a good speller and "sort of scribbled" to hide the spelling mistakes. The teacher gave him a list of spelling rules, and Andrew bought a spelling dictionary which he was permitted to use during tests and examinations. As well, he began typing his assignments and found that the spell check helped his spelling because he could see the correct version. He discovered, too, that the neat, typewritten pages looked much better than the handwritten versions so he started putting them into plastic covers instead of just stapling them.

> Students like positive feedback that acknowledges their good work. For older students, write comments on the last page of a submitted assignment. Your comments can be on the work, as well as on any positive behaviors in which you have noticed an improvement, such as submission of assignments.

The teacher asked Andrew to monitor his attendance, late arrivals, bringing of a notebook and pen, and submission of assignments. She did the same. Since the middle of October, he skipped only one class (the day before the Christmas holidays) and was late for three (all in October and early November). While doing the self-monitoring, Andrew was amazed at how often he thought about skipping, particularly in October and early November, but he knew his parents would be telephoned immediately and decided to go to class. On the three occasions where he was late, he seriously thought of skipping, but changed his mind.

In case students such as Andrew forgot basic classroom tools, the teacher was ready. She always kept extra looseleaf paper in the classroom and gave Andrew a sheet or two when necessary. If he forgot his pen, she loaned him one. However, in order to receive a loaner, he had to surrender his bus pass for the period. She extended this policy to all students and found that it had the greatest effect on those who had to give a shoe as collateral. Once was all it took to have those students find a pen to bring to class. At the end of each week, she and Andrew met quickly after class (which was just before lunch) and examined tally charts.

*Decision*
- referred for testing for possible learning disability in area of written expression
- special education department will monitor and second semester teachers will continue using these adaptations

Andrew's parents had agreed to have him tested as it was suspected that he might have a mild learning disability; however, that wouldn't occur until April.

Meanwhile, the teacher was implementing accommodations that were designed to teach Andrew how to cope with his writing problems (through organizing his thoughts before writing and using the computer) and to use his relatively strong oral abilities whenever possible. By the end of the semester, his mark in English had risen to 64 percent from 52 percent, in large part due to the marks accumulated through oral presentations. Although his written work was legible, his ideas were still not fully expressed. This area required further work which would be done after the results of formal testing were made available.

With the help of his teacher and parents, Andrew was finally taking responsibility for his work. However, this change in behavior might not have occurred if Andrew had not been "ready" to make some changes. Last fall he felt that his marks in English were so low his parents would be very upset. He was thus motivated to try the teacher's plan in order to avoid punishment. He had been successful at submitting typewritten assignments and doing work orally. As well, his attendance was no longer a problem, and he was bringing his notebook and pen to class. The teacher's hunch had been correct: Andrew would attend classes if he knew he could be successful.

At the beginning of the second semester, the English teacher, the special education teacher, the parents, Andrew, and Andrew's new teachers met. The English teacher gave them a copy of the planning sheet she had prepared (see pages 35 and 36), described the accommodations she had implemented, and outlined the progress Andrew had made. It was decided that the special education teacher would monitor Andrew's progress and work with the new teachers. Andrew's parents again expressed their gratitude, and Andrew mumbled something about English not being that bad after all.

## The Value of Positive Reinforcement

ALEX

At the initial meeting with the parents, it became known that Alex was greatly distressed about her father's medical condition. It appeared that this anxiety had likely triggered the girl's increasingly disruptive behaviors. However, when the teacher spoke to the special education teacher about possible techniques for use with Alex, it became painfully obvious to her that she should alter her teaching approach. She realized that she was too rigid and too talkative and that she was not providing the kind of structure that Alex (and a few other children) needed. She felt that she was too quick to become angry and punish Alex. In short, the teacher realized that *she* would have to make some changes to her teaching style that might benefit everyone.

### Addressing behavior problems

The teacher planned the next social studies unit using centres at which the children moved about the room in groups and wrote answers to questions, dramatized certain events, drew pictures, made maps, and did some research using books and the Internet. Setting up the activities at the centres and tracking the students' work were time consuming, but the children were able to move about and the teacher could monitor Alex's behavior.

# Planning Sheet

NAME: *Andrew*                         IMPLEMENTATION DATE: *October*

GRADE: *9*

STRENGTHS

– *participates in oral discussions*
– *is able to express his ideas well orally*

WEAKNESSES

– *arrives late (4) and skips class (up to 10)*
– *easily off-task*
– *refuses to complete some assignments or portions of some assignments*
– *hands in assignments late (7/9 were late)*
– *doesn't always bring his notebook and pen to class (6 times in 6 weeks)*
– *written assignments too short*
– *handwriting very messy*

## GOALS

1. *To lengthen written responses*
2. *To improve neatness of written work*

## ADAPTATIONS

1. *Length of Written Assignments*
   – *use the Frame for Writing a Five-Paragraph Essay for five-paragraph essays and work individually with Andrew*
   – *provide samples of completed assignments*
   – *discuss the answers to questions about the novel, short story, poem etc. before he writes the answers*
   – *give extensions if required*
   – *occasionally organize assignments to give a choice to respond orally*

2. *Neatness of Written Assignments*
   – *encourage Andrew to write on every second line and to space out letters of words*
   – *inform all students as to when the school's computer lab is open*
   – *encourage Andrew to type assignments*

3. *Other*
   – *accommodations for tests and exams — point form, extra time, part written and part oral*
   – *encourage Andrew to participate in group discussions*
   – *seat Andrew close to the front to monitor off-task behaviors*
   – *set up a chart for Andrew so that he can keep a tally count of lates, skipping, bringing notebook and pen, submitting assignments*
   – *have looseleaf paper available*
   – *loan a pen with collateral*
   – *praise Andrew discreetly for submitting assignments on time, etc.*
   – *develop a rapport with Andrew*

**POST-IMPLEMENTATION RESULTS:**   *February*

1.  *Length of Written Assignments*
    – the writing frame helped him organize ideas
    – he needed only one extension between mid-November and January
    – chose to do as many assignments orally as possible
    – extra time given for the exam, tests answered in point form — effective
    – assignments were longer, but not substantially
    – mark rose from 52% to 64%

2.  *Neatness of Written Assignments*
    – typing the assignments and using the spell check feature helped
    – it was detected that Andrew is not a competent speller — uses a spelling dictionary

3.  *Other*
    – tally sheets helped him monitor his own behaviors
    – having looseleaf to give and pens to loan helped

## DECISION
– referred for testing for possible learning disability in area of written expression
– special education department will monitor and second semester teachers will continue using these adaptations

Classroom rules should be expressed as positively as possible. For example:

1. Respect yourself.
2. Respect others.
3. Respect the property of others.

However, some students need more specific instructions, such as "keep your hands and feet to yourself." These may be expressed either positively or negatively *using a calm voice.* A threatening voice doesn't work because a student may see this as a challenge that must be taken up.

During other times of the day, the teacher adopted task analysis (see pages 75–76) because it made a job seem less big and overwhelming to Alex. As Alex completed each section of the assignment, she was rewarded with praise and the opportunity to get a drink. Every time Alex went for a drink, the teacher reminded her of the rules (no talking and no touching). A few times Alex's drink privileges were suspended because she talked with or touched another child. However, for the most part, this technique worked.

Alex and her teacher each tallied the number of times per day that she was out of her seat without the teacher's permission. Alex was surprised that she was wandering so often and made the link between wandering and being able to finish her work in school as opposed to at home. Once she realized the relationship, she tried harder to stay on task and in her seat. Alex and her teacher decided that she could be out of her seat (other than with the teacher's permission) five times a day. She was fairly successful at this, and by the middle of February was receiving stickers every day in her planner. Her parents rewarded her with a double-scoop, chocolate-dipped ice-cream cone at the mall on Friday if she received stickers every day that week.

The teacher provided a second desk for Alex at the back of the room where she could do her seatwork. After two weeks Alex begged the teacher to move her closer to some of the other children, and that lasted two days. Before the teacher moved her back, Alex had pushed her new desk to its previous position. She explained that she was talking too much, walking around, and not getting her work done. She had missed a day's sticker and knew her parents were disappointed. However, she joined in group work which had been structured so that there were many opportunities for discussion. The teacher monitored Alex's group closely to ensure that the students' discussions remained on topic.

The teacher also watched for signs of agitation in Alex and tried to de-escalate conflict by using the "broken record" technique. She was amazed that the technique worked. She noted when Alex was becoming tired and angry, and tried to monitor the girl's behaviors *before* they got out of hand. She used proximity control (see page 70) and provided Alex with as much individual attention as she could give.

The teacher offered more choice in some activities, which Alex and others appreciated.

However, one major incident occurred during the first week in February. Alex refused to do her math assignment, yelled and screamed, threw her pencil on the floor, and ran out of the classroom. The teacher followed her outside of the classroom to find her crying uncontrollably. When Alex had calmed down enough to talk, the teacher learned that her father was undergoing exploratory surgery. Alex was afraid that he would die. Since the meeting with the parents, Alex's mother and father had explained the heart condition and the operation to her, and Alex had seemed less anxious about it. Nonetheless, Alex's mother had sent a note to the teacher forewarning her about possible problems the day of the operation. Alex had forgotten to give the note to the teacher. In the hallway, Alex said that she was too embarrassed to return to the classroom and wanted to do her work at the office. The teacher made the arrangements, and Alex worked quietly in the office until lunch, then returned to the class. The teacher made certain that no comments about the incident were made to Alex by the other children.

## Revisiting classroom management and instructional practices

Besides planning more movement in her lessons, the teacher sought to make the instructional part shorter and to involve the children more. She incorporated more questioning, the use of manipulatives in math, hands-on work in science, and variety in her lessons. The teacher also revamped her classroom management and discipline techniques.

The teacher recognized that, when calling on children to answer questions, she hadn't always followed the hands-up rule herself. She would invite the children to raise their hands, then ask someone who hadn't raised a hand. The teacher realized that her own behavior may have contributed to Alex's habit of blurting out answers. Therefore, she began following the rule consistently. She stated the hands-up rule and called only on those students who raised their hands. She called on Alex as soon as hers was raised to reinforce the link between hands up and answering. She also tried to cue Alex about raising her hand by tapping her own right hand with her left index finger. By the end of March, Alex was blurting out answers only one or two times per lesson. The teacher also used group praise ("I like the way you are raising your hands") which seemed to reinforce this behavior for everyone.

The teacher realized that she should be calmer and more assertive instead of becoming angry. She found that using "I-messages" and offering choices about behavior ("If you choose to leave your seat one more time, you will lose your sticker for the day") helped her remain calm. She also stopped yelling at Alex as this made both of them angry. It was better to monitor Alex, watch for signs of agitation, provide a few seconds of individual attention, and praise for staying on task. Finally, in an effort to develop a rapport with Alex, the teacher made a point of talking to the girl each day about non-school matters. She learned that Alex had recently done well at a swim meet and that her name was in the newspaper. The teacher cut out the article, and with Alex's permission tacked it on the bulletin board. She was permitting herself to develop a positive attitude towards her student.

At the end of March the teacher invited Alex, her parents, the special education teacher, and the principal in for a second meeting. She described the outcomes of the plan and stated that Alex's disruptive behaviors had decreased and that academically she was doing above average work. Alex's mother reported that Alex had seemed happier at home and was no longer showing the aggressive behaviors towards her younger brother. Her mother explained that at home they were trying to help Alex use her words to express anger instead of showing it through physical means. She also said that Alex did enjoy the ice-cream cones and that chocolate and ice cream were strong motivators for her daughter. Alex's father reported that all had gone well with the exploratory surgery, and he had resumed his normal activities. The anxiety everyone had felt about his health had subsided. It was decided to continue the plan until the end of the year, as Alex was proud of the stickers and wanted the weekly ice-cream cone. It was also decided that the special education teacher and the classroom teacher would discuss the plan with Alex's Grade 6 teacher next fall.

---

An important skill for teachers to learn is how to work with one child at her desk and still watch the other students. I try to position myself in such a way that I have my back to the least number of students, watch the ones in front of me, and turn around periodically to monitor those behind me.

*Decision*
– continue the plan until June
– special education teacher and Grade 5 teacher will meet with Grade 6 teacher in the fall

# Planning Sheet

NAME: *Alex*                    IMPLEMENTATION DATE: *November*

GRADE: *5*

STRENGTHS                                      WEAKNESSES

– *athletic; is on swim team*                  – *out of seat 15–17 times a day*
– *vivid imagination; writes well*             – *talks constantly*
                                           – *blurts out answers 4–7 times a day*
                                           – *short attention span*
                                           – *argues*

## GOALS

1.  *To decrease the out-of-seat behaviors*
2.  *To decrease the talking*
3.  *To decrease the arguing*

## ADAPTATIONS

1.  *Wandering*
    – *plan lessons that allow some movement in the classroom*
    – *use task analysis to break an assignment into smaller pieces, praise when each segment is completed, reward with the opportunity to get a drink*
    – *have Alex monitor her own behavior using tally counts for number of times she is out of her seat*
    – *establish a number of times each day that she may be out of her seat without the teacher's permission*
    – *reteach the classroom rules about moving in the room*

2.  *Constant Talking*
    – *assign Alex one desk at the front of the room and a second one at the back of the classroom*
    – *plan more lessons involving group work where talking wouldn't be disruptive and might be focused on the task*

3.  *Arguing*
    – *provide more choices in classroom work*
    – *use the "broken record" technique in response to arguing*

4.  *Other*
    – *enforce the "hands up" rule when calling on students to answer a question*
    – *use non-verbal cues to remind Alex to raise her hand or to return to her seat*
    – *plan interesting lessons in which movement, manipulating objects, and discussion are included*
    – *use a multisensory method of teaching in which instruction is presented using the visual, auditory, kinesthetic, and tactile channels*
    – *use "I-messages" when Alex does not follow the rules*
    – *monitor Alex in the classroom*
    – *provide as much individual attention as possible*

- give Alex opportunities to "shine"
- develop a rapport with Alex

**POST-IMPLEMENTATION RESULTS:** *March*

1. *Wandering*
   - using centres helped to provide Alex with opportunities to move; monitoring of her behavior was possible
   - task analysis worked — the assignment didn't seem so overwhelming and she was motivated to do the work and get the drink
   - self-monitoring of wandering helped her realize how often she was out of her seat — effective because it helped her make a link between wandering and completion of work
   - reward program with stickers was successful; most of the time not out of seat without permission more than five times a day

2. *Constant Talking*
   - the desk at the back worked, less talking; working at the back of the classroom was not viewed as a punishment
   - group discussions were successful

3. *Arguing*
   - choice was given in lessons and units — Alex appreciated this
   - the "broken-record" technique worked and helped to de-escalate the conflict
   - proximity control and individual attention helped keep Alex focused

4. *Other*
   - reducing the instruction portion of the lesson and involving Alex in the lesson helped to maintain Alex's attention
   - enforced the "hands up" rule, group praise, and cuing were successful with all of the children, blurting out answers only 1–2 times per lesson
   - monitoring Alex's levels of agitation, individual attention, and praise helped to stop a conflict before it started
   - use of "I-messages" and giving choices about behavior
   - Alex enjoyed the conversations before school

**DECISION**

- continue the plan until June
- special education teacher and Grade 5 teacher will meet with Grade 6 teacher in the fall

# Opportunities to Shine

ERIK

A case conference is an *informal* meeting between the school staff, the parents, and the student to discuss the student's progress and ways to improve it.

A week after the September Grade 7 staff meeting, at which Erik's computer, math, and music abilities were noted, a case conference was set up with Erik and his parents, the homeroom teacher, the music teacher, the vice-principal, and the special education teacher. It was decided that Erik would not be referred for testing, but that accommodations would be made.

Between October and June, Erik took advantage of many opportunities presented to him. His homeroom teacher, also the supervisor of the Engineering Club, informed the entire class of the meetings. He then privately invited Erik to attend. Erik was initially shy about going, being a Grade 7 student mixing with some high school students, but he met another Grade 7 boy who shared his interests and they became "regulars." He enjoyed the problem solving, learned how to upgrade his family's computer, and discovered more about careers in engineering and in the high tech sector. As well, he attended the enrichment camp held at the local university and spent the week in the new technology faculty. Finally, the teacher began having the students do daily brain teasers and a longer problem to be solved by the end of the week for a mark out of 5. Erik enjoyed these questions and noticed how popular he was by Thursday as the weekly questions were due on Fridays. In the area of computers, Erik did three extra projects, one of which was entered into the school's science fair. He was awarded second prize for the intermediate students. (A Grade 8 student won.)

Very few children are *globally gifted*, meaning that they excel in all academic areas. These children are usually provided with an enrichment program at school. However, some students have a gift in just one area, which also needs special nourishment.

In music Erik really shone. Although he had never had musical training other than singing in the elementary schools he attended, he became passionate about the saxophone. He happily practised at home and finished the Grade 7 book by the end of March. The music teacher gave him extra sheet music and started him on the Grade 8 book in April. Erik joined the Grade 7 Band and met more friends. In the early spring Erik began practising with the Grade 8 Jazz Band, and he was amazed to learn that they would be competing in a local festival.

*Decision*
– individual ability testing will not be done
– special education department will monitor Eric's progress and will inform future teachers
– continue using the planning form to organize accommodations

At a case conference at the end of the year, Erik and his parents decided against testing. Erik clearly had gifts in math, computers, and music, but to be admitted into a gifted program a student needed to have a global IQ score of at least the 98 percentile. With Erik's only above average marks in English, his composite score was unlikely to be that high. As well, Erik didn't want to move to another school where the gifted program was offered as he had just made some friends. He didn't want to have to break into a new social scene. He did want to continue with the Engineering Club, the Grade 8 Band, and the Jazz Band next year.

It was decided that the special education teacher would monitor Erik's progress over the next few years and would inform future teachers about some of the ways the program could be enriched. Although an IEP was not written, the planning sheet developed by the homeroom and music teachers became the reference point for making accommodations for Erik.

Meanwhile, Erik's parents had quietly been searching for appropriate summer camps for their son. They had found one camp in computers at the university and a jazz camp offered by a community group. These were both weeklong day camps, which Erik agreed to attend. Erik's parents had also looked into private saxophone lessons which would begin the following September.

# Planning Sheet

NAME: *Erik*                    IMPLEMENTATION DATE: *October*

GRADE: *7*

STRENGTHS                        WEAKNESSES

– *math and computers*
– *music*

## GOALS

1. *Math and Computers*
   – *encourage Erik to join the Engineering Club*
   – *provide enrichment activities in class and ask open-ended questions*
   – *encourage Erik to do one extra project in computers, which would be entered in the school's Science Fair*

2. *Music*
   – *encourage Erik to join the Grade 7 Band*
   – *work at his own pace through the Grade 7 music book, offer tutoring, give sheet music of more challenging pieces*
   – *informally acknowledge him as the first saxophonist of the Grade 7 Band, find pieces for the saxophones*
   – *possibly encourage him to join the Jazz Band*
   – *speak to Erik's parents about private lessons*

3. *Other*
   – *encourage Erik to attend the enrichment camp held at the university each spring*

## POST-IMPLEMENTATION RESULTS:  *June*

1. *Math and Computers*
   – *did join the Engineering Club, participated in contests*
   – *did three extra projects in computers, one was entered in the Science Fair (Second Prize)*
   – *enjoyed the enrichment questions*

2. *Music*
   – *joined the Grade 7 Band*
   – *finished the Grade 7 book in March, began working on the Grade 8 book in April*
   – *joined the Jazz Band*

## DECISION

– *individual ability testing will not be done*
– *special education department will monitor Erik's progress and will inform future teachers*
– *continue using the planning form to organize accommodations*

# Distilling Key Principles from the Case Studies

Two important principles can be derived from the case studies presented. They should guide our attitudes and actions regarding all students and, in particular, those who require accommodations in our classrooms. These principles can be summarized as follows: (1) work with others and (2) caring teachers can make a difference.

## Work with others

Given the range of student abilities and needs, it is impossible for one person to meet all of those needs effectively. You will have to enlist the support of colleagues, the students' parents, the child, and such school personnel as the principal. Know and draw upon the skills and experiences of others as you work cooperatively with colleagues and parents.

As was shown in each of the case studies, the teachers discussed their observations and ideas about possible accommodations with the special education teacher. The special education teacher can provide valuable ideas about how to make minor adaptations to your teaching style and curriculum.

A second source of support is a child's parents. In each of the case studies, the parents provided either active or moral support for the work of the teacher. Most often, parents are grateful that a teacher has made certain observations and is willing to implement a plan to assist their child. The importance of the home and school working together in providing remediation, a supportive environment, or enrichment for a child can't be emphasized enough.

The third partner is the child, who will either accept the assistance or reject it. In all case studies presented here, the students were willing to collaborate, and in one case, the student wanted to be an equal partner in the development of the "extra work." An old maxim states that you can lead a horse to water, but you can't make it drink. This saying is particularly appropriate when working with teens and pre-teens who often worry about being perceived as different from their peers. The adaptations for these students must be fully acceptable to them; otherwise, the students will not cooperate.

The final partner consists of school personnel, such as the principal, who may provide moral support for your work; other teachers, who will join you in implementing accommodations for a student; paraprofessionals, who may be available to assist you in putting into practice certain programs; and other professionals, such as a speech language pathologist, who can provide information and ideas. Therefore, although the classroom teacher takes the lead role in making the adaptations, the success of the plan frequently depends on the teacher's ability to work with others.

## Caring teachers can make a difference

In each of the case studies, it was an observant and caring teacher who initiated a plan and guided its implementation. As a caring professional who is concerned about maximizing the learning of all students, you, too, can make observations, develop a plan of action, put it into practice, and make it work. Doing this involves time, energy, and a commitment to providing the best possible opportunities for each child.

Caring teachers, such as those who taught Andrew, Alex, and Erik, look beyond the delivery of the curriculum to review the performance of each student and consider ways of making it better. In other words, they look beyond their own needs and examine the needs of others. They reflect on their own practices and decide what is helping children learn and what is not. They have the courage to abandon those practices that are not working and seek better ones. They also take the time to work with others on developing adaptations, to make adjustments in their teaching methods and curriculum, and to do follow-up on students' progress. The fact that you are reading this book suggests that you are one of them.

The keys to working with at-risk and exceptional children are easily stated. First, you need a sense of commitment to children and to the teaching profession. Next, you need to take the time to make observations, develop a plan, implement it, and do the follow-up. Finally, you have to be a sufficiently flexible thinker to see the possibilities for each child instead of just the problems they create for you.

These ideas are easily stated, but not always easily implemented. Success depends not only on you, but the child, the parents, and other people in the school. Is it worth the effort of striving to meet the special needs of your students? Of course, it is. But it takes a caring teacher to initiate the process and adopt appropriate teaching practices and accommodations. Some of these are outlined in Part B.

# Summary Checklist for Working with a Student Whose Exceptionalities Have Not Yet Been Identified

Identify and systematically observe any student whose academic performance is well above or below the standard or whose behavior is inappropriate over a period of time.

## 1. Making Observations

❏ Collect data on the student's strengths.

❏ Collect data on the student's weaknesses.

## 2. Formulating Goals

❏ Prioritize areas to be remediated.

❏ Decide on areas for enrichment.

❏ Decide which behaviors to modify.

## 3. Developing Adaptations

❏ Meet with the special education teacher.

❏ Develop accommodations.

❏ Meet with the parents, the student, the special education teacher, and the school administration.

❏ Decide on a time frame to try the accommodations.

## 4. Implementing and Reviewing the Action Plan

❏ Implement the plan.

❏ Collect data on the areas to be remediated.

❏ Collect data on the areas for enrichment.

❏ Meet with the parents, the student, the special education teacher, and the school administration.

❏ Decide on the next steps.

# Exceptionalities and How to Work with Students Who Have Them

# CHAPTER 5

# Learning Disabilities

In discussing learning disabilities, a definition of exclusion is used: learning disabilities are *not* primarily the result of impairment of vision, impairment of hearing, physical disability, intellectual disability, primary emotional disturbance, or cultural difference. However, a learning disability results in significant discrepancy between academic achievement and assessed intellectual ability, with deficits in one or more of the following: receptive language, language processing, expressive language, or mathematical computations. Dyslexia, perhaps the word most often associated with learning disabilities, is a particular type of disability that relates to a person's ability to read, spell, and write.

After almost four decades of discussion, there is no universal agreement on how to classify the problems that come under the general term *learning disability*. Psychologists focus on dysfunctions in areas such as perception, processing, memory, and attention. Medical researchers emphasize genetics and brain organization and function. And teachers zero in on academic difficulties. Despite this lack of agreement, the primary causes of learning disabilities have been identified.

## Causes of Learning Disabilities

Some children develop at a slower rate, and consequently they are unable to do the expected work. Eventually, their achievement profile may resemble that of a person with learning disabilities: scores in reading and math that are two years below grade level. However, these students may not have a learning disability. With remedial assistance they may be able to improve their scores.

Experts agree that learning is hindered because the brain has a problem in the way it processes information. Why it does is unknown. Several causes of learning disabilities are outlined below.

*Nervous System Disorders:* Some children with normal vision and hearing may misinterpret everyday sights and sounds due to some unexplained disorder of the nervous system. Researchers postulate that learning disabilities are linked to a problem in the brain's wiring that interferes with the ability to function. For example, studies have shown that adults with dyslexia show greater than normal activity in the visual areas of the brain when reading than in the auditory sections of the brain. People without dyslexia show widespread activity in both the sight and hearing areas of the brain.

*Head Injuries and Illnesses:* Some learning disabilities are accounted for by head injuries at birth and in childhood. Illnesses or disorders linked to learning problems are high fever, encephalitis, meningitis, and diabetes.

*Premature Births:* Children born prematurely and children who had medical problems soon after birth sometimes have learning disabilities.

*Genetic Factors:* Genetic makeup can make a child vulnerable to developing learning disabilities, which are then triggered by an environmental factor, such as birth trauma. However, there is strong evidence that learning disabilities that involve reading problems (dyslexia) can be passed from one generation to the next. Chromosome 15 has been related to dyslexia, particularly in the development of word identification, and chromosome 6 is linked to phonological segmentation, or the ability to divide a word into its sounds.

## Types of Learning Disabilities

The academic areas that serve to identify students with learning disabilities can be summarized as reading, written expression, and math.

### Reading

Can dyslexics be helped? With early intervention, some people can improve their reading abilities. However, poor reading is likely to be a lifelong condition.

Reading disabilities are often referred to as *dyslexia.* They reflect a persistent deficit rather than a developmental lag. Lyon (1995) found that of those children who were reading disabled in Grade 3, approximately 74 percent continue to read significantly below grade level in Grade 9. Hence, dyslexia is generally a condition that a person does *not* grow out of. People with dyslexia often have difficulty decoding words and are unable to identify the main idea of a passage. Some adults learn to compensate for their inability to identify the main idea of a passage by drawing on their previous life experiences to bring meaning to it (Kintsch, 1990). People with dyslexia may also experience difficulty recalling basic facts and events in a sequence, and making inferences or evaluating what they have read. As many females as males manifest dyslexia; however, schools identify three to four times more boys than girls, largely through initial observations of behavior problems.

Here's how a person with dyslexia typically fares with the four steps in the reading process.

1. *Phonological awareness* is an understanding that words are made up of different sounds (44 in English). It also involves the ability to segment words and syllables into sounds or phonemes. The ability to decode single words accurately and fluently is dependent upon this ability to divide words into their basic sounds.

   Many dyslexics lack phonological awareness and are unable to segment words into phonemes. For example, they may not understand that the word "bat" is made up of three sounds, "b," "a," and "t." Instead, a person with dyslexia may perceive the word as having one sound. For an undetermined reason, the brain of a person with dyslexia is unable to translate a written word into units of sounds, or phonemes. Hence, a person with dyslexia attempts to read relying heavily on his or her visual memory rather than on auditory abilities.

2. Phonics involves linking sounds to letters of the alphabet (sound/symbol association). This process can be confusing for some people as the English language has many letters and letter combinations that have multiple sounds. For example, the letter "c" has a "k" sound in "cup," but an "s" sound in "ice." Longitudinal data shows that dyslexic readers benefit from one-to-one instruction in phonics rather than being immersed in a whole language approach only.

3. When sound/symbol association becomes automatic, the decoding of words becomes fast and accurate. However, some dyslexic readers take more time than the average reader to develop the links between sounds and letters and may never become fast readers who correctly read every word.

4. Comprehending a passage depends on the ability to decode words rapidly and accurately. A fluent reader focuses on the meaning of the words rather than what the individual words are. People with dyslexia spend so much time and effort decoding words that they can't focus on the meaning of a passage; they read words, rather than extracting meaning from the text. As well, some dyslexic readers find it difficult to identify the main idea due to their poor ability to think abstractly and to organize their thoughts.

### Speaking and listening

Language deficits are found in the areas of oral expression (speaking) and listening comprehension. Common oral language problems include difficulty in coming up with the right word (word retrieval), slowness in answering questions, and the use of simpler structures and words in sentences than that of peers. A child with learning disabilities may process language more slowly than others or may misinterpret the meaning of the message. Not following instructions, appearing to be balky, or daydreaming, and the like may be misinterpreted as behavioral issues rather than as listening difficulties. Students with learning disabilities may also miss nonverbal cues and may not understand jokes which can contribute to difficulties in social situations.

### Mathematics

*Dyscalculia* refers to a learning disability related to problems making math calculations and reasoning. Students may have difficulty understanding and working with the four operations, the concept of zero, regrouping, place value, and basic math concepts (e.g., one-to-one correspondence, sets), as well as solving math problems (Smith, Polloway, Dowdy, & Blalock, 1997).

Dyscalculia is sometimes accompanied by visual-motor problems, which make it difficult for the student to pick up and count manipulatives. As well, visual perception problems may make it hard for a student to align numbers in columns, copy numbers correctly, or see an inscribed triangle. Finally, a person with dyscalculia may reverse numbers (e.g., 23 instead of 32).

### Writing

A person with learning disabilities may have *dysgraphia*, which refers to problems in printing or cursive writing. Writing may be labored, slow, messy, and illegible, reflecting poorly developed fine-motor skills. Some students with learning disabilities also experience persistent difficulties with spelling and written expression (including creativity, grammar, and sentence structure).

## The Effects of Learning Disabilities on General Academic Performance

Although the primary characteristic of a learning disability is a significant difference between a child's achievement and overall intelligence as measured by an individually administered IQ test (usually the WISC III), learning disabilities typically affect these general areas:

- Spoken language: delays or disorders in speech and language; problems in expressing ideas in speech
- Written language: difficulties with reading (decoding, main idea), spelling, and writing (written expression or handwriting)
- Arithmetic: difficulty in performing arithmetic operations or understanding basic concepts
- Reasoning: difficulty in organizing and integrating thoughts; may demonstrate limited vocabulary, little ability to think abstractly, problems in identifying similarities and differences, or few age-appropriate social-cognitive abilities
- Memory: difficulty in remembering information and instruction in written or oral form; problems in sequencing
- Spatial: problems with visual discrimination, laterality (distinguishing left from right), telling time using an analogue clock, fine- and gross-motor coordination, and body image
- Attention: inability to concentrate for long periods; easily distracted
- Performance: inconsistent, that is, knows something one day but not the next

## Characteristics of Elementary Students with Learning Disabilities

Every student with a learning disability will have an individual profile of strengths and weaknesses. In other words, every case is different. However, a general rule when identifying learning disabilities is that there is a significant difference between performance and potential. If you suspect a student of having a learning disability, you need to observe the child over time to determine frequency and clusters of certain behaviors. Be sure to record your observations in a private journal or on a checklist.

Your observations may be important in initiating the assessment process, which may result in determining that a child has a learning disability. In many districts, a student must be identified before extra support will be provided. The identification process typically involves (1) the classroom teacher who makes informal observations, (2) the special education teacher who does a screening assessment, and (3) the psychologist who administers an individual IQ test. The results of the IQ test are examined for strengths and significant weaknesses and are compared to the student's academic achievement.

The following characteristics will not be demonstrated by every student with a learning disability: each child demonstrates specific clusters of characteristics.

# What to Look for in Students Suspected of Having a Learning Disability

## ELEMENTARY STUDENTS

### Reading

- ❏ difficulty in segmenting the sounds of a word
- ❏ problems in associating sounds and letters
- ❏ loses place regularly (tracking problem)
- ❏ makes "wild" guesses (comprehension)
- ❏ does not attempt to decode a word and looks at the teacher
- ❏ ignores punctuation and other cues
- ❏ makes up words and inserts them into the passage
- ❏ reverses the letters of words (e.g., *was* and *saw*)
- ❏ transposes words (changes the order of the words in a passage)
- ❏ loses meaning of a sentence from beginning to end
- ❏ has difficulty sequencing events in a story
- ❏ makes incorrect inferences
- ❏ does not identify the main idea
- ❏ identifies only a few supporting details

### Work Speed

- ❏ frequently does not complete the written work
- ❏ works more slowly than age and grade peers
- ❏ has difficulty beginning a task
- ❏ is frustrated under time pressure

### Work with the Alphabet and Penmanship

- ❏ may confuse letters in recitation and writing
- ❏ mixes lower and upper case letters
- ❏ mixes manuscript and cursive styles, or will continue to use manuscript long after peers use cursive
- ❏ has poor printing or handwriting: may be illegible
- ❏ often mirrors or reverses letters
- ❏ shows awkward movement of a pencil or pen

### Remembering

- ❏ often forgets or misplaces things
- ❏ needs constant reminding (and has often trained family, teachers, or friends to do this)
- ❏ may know something one day but not the next

### Time and Sequence

- ❑ displays a poor notion of chronological order
- ❑ tends not to see time in discrete units
- ❑ may be unable to tell time using an analogue clock
- ❑ has difficulty following a set of instructions (may follow them out of sequence or with sections missing)

### Spelling

- ❑ uses creative spelling long past his or her peers
- ❑ does not seem to retain a basic stock of spelling words

### Copying/Notetaking

- ❑ loses place often
- ❑ often inaccurate; omits sections, subheadings

### Arithmetic

- ❑ reverses numbers long past his or her peers
- ❑ unable to align numbers in columns
- ❑ unable to remember addition, subtraction, multiplication, and division facts
- ❑ carries or borrows the wrong digit
- ❑ has difficulty following steps in long division
- ❑ has difficulty understanding the concept of zero
- ❑ finds it hard to understand place value
- ❑ has difficulty with problem solving

No student will exhibit all of the above characteristics. However, *clusters* of behaviors that are displayed *frequently* and *over time* may indicate that a child has a learning disability.

# Ways to Help Elementary Students Learn

## Reading skills

*Basic Skills:* The first step in learning how to read is to understand that letters and words have sounds; therefore, it is important to work on phonological awareness. Teach rhyming words, have the students listen to rhyming words, and prompt them to say their own rhyming words. As children become familiar with the concept of rhyming, pause before each rhyming word to allow them to predict what the next word might be. Next, teach segmenting sentences into words and words into syllables. Use woodsticks, blocks, or counters to hit or point to as each word in a sentence or syllable in a word or sentence is said. Then, move on to identifying the sounds within words. For initial, ending, and middle sounds, teach the sounds, then delete the sound, and substitute the sound. Then teach the sounds of blended letters: for example, cl-a-p has three sounds.

Immerse the children in the printed word by reading to them everyday, labelling classroom objects, and displaying books and other printed materials, such as a phone book, in the classroom.

Create a word bank for the children to assist them in their writing. The words may be generated through discussions with your students or may be from word lists that accompany your reading series. Write the words on paper, cut them out, and tack them on a wall or chalkboard. They may be arranged alphabetically or by category, such as nouns or verbs. You may want to write these words on small cards so that pairs of children can use them as a drill activity where one child says the words to a partner.

Another technique is to write sentences on strips of chart paper, using key vocabulary words. The children then read the strips. The words in the strips can also be cut, and the children can assemble sentences in a logical order and read them. The strategy here is to give children many opportunities to read; repetition is the key to learning.

*Advanced Skills:* The focus of your accommodations is on helping students understand the story or novel. Do your best to select a novel or story that will interest the students. If you have novel groups, choose high interest, low vocabulary novels for the weak readers. Pre-reading activities could include teaching the key vocabulary so that the children will recognize the words and understand what they mean. As well, discuss previous experiences or knowledge that will give the students a context for the story and a basis for understanding.

During the reading of the novel or story, permit students to read while listening to an audiotape of the passage. Listening to the tape speeds the reading process, improves comprehension, and increases attention span. Sometimes, the tapes are available commercially; however, you usually have to record them yourself.

After reading the story or chapter, discuss the story with the students to ensure understanding of plot, characters, setting, and so on. Then ask the students to write their responses to the questions on these story elements. Introducing scaffolds would help the students organize the parts of the novel or story. *Scaffolding* is a technique that helps students move from working with direct assistance to working independently. An example of a scaffold, or support, is a form with key words or headings that help the students organize their ideas. The scaffold provides indirect support for the student through the key words, which act as prompts. For a novel or story, a chart with the following headings could be made: Setting, Main Characters, and Plot, which could have the subheadings Introduction, Rising Action, Climax, Falling Action, and Resolution. The students then write points under each heading either at the end of the novel or as you read each chapter.

### Spelling

Select a spelling series that focuses on word families. Through the repetition of word families, such as "ight," the students will see patterns that may be applied to their everyday spelling. As well, some students may need a *multisensory* method of teaching. You could write the words on chart paper and introduce them by reading them aloud and pointing to them. Then have the students say the words as you point to them. Discuss the words and look for similarities and differences. Highlight these with different colored markers. Have the children write the words in their notebooks. Finally, ask them to trace the letters of the words using Scrabble tiles or laminated letters.

For spelling tests, some of your students may require a reduction in the number of words learned each week. You may find that a student can only manage 10 of 20 words. When dictating the words, break the words into syllables so that the students can focus on small chunks of the word at a time. For example, if the word is "computer," say the whole word first. Then say *com*, then *put*, and finally *er*. Say the word again without breaking it into syllables. This is the *whole-part-whole* method. When pencil is not permitted, encourage the students to use erasable pens. When marking the spelling test, award two points per word: two points, if the word is perfect; and one point, if the word is incorrect but the student can correct it. Indicate the score as a portion of a whole, for example, 16/20 instead of so many wrong.

Encourage your students to use spelling aids. For everyday spelling, let them use a spelling dictionary (either commercial or personal), a thesaurus, and perhaps an electronic spelling device (a calculator-sized device). Encourage them to learn how to type their projects. There are many software programs that teach keyboarding. As well, teach them to use the spell-check feature on the computer. Using the computer for assignments, such as stories, will increase the number of correctly spelled words. It may also improve the students' spelling as they see that their version is not correct and discover how to spell the word correctly.

### Printing and handwriting

When teaching printing, use the *continuous flow* method instead of the ball and stick method. With the continuous flow method, the student does not have to lift the pencil — the alternative is drawing a circle, lifting the pencil, and trying to draw the line so that it touches the ball. Students experiencing delays in fine-motor development or who have deficits in visual-spatial abilities find the continuous flow method easier to do than the other.

When teaching a specific letter, such as "a," do pre-writing activities: for example, saying the name of the letter, listening to and producing the sound of the letter, noting how the mouth feels when saying the letter, and brainstorming words that begin with "a." Then print an "a" on chart paper or the board, then another "a" while you describe your motions, and then a final "a." When breaking the instruction into parts for the letter "a," you might say: "We begin our circle at the 2 o'clock position (point to the clock so that the students can see the 2). Curve to the left and make sure the bottom of the circle touches the

To improve word recognition, teach the child to look for familiar parts in multisyllabic words. For example, "returned" may be segmented into the prefix, root, and suffix: *re turn ed*. The child would find the familiar parts and put them together when sounding out the word. As well, provide lists of grade-appropriate words or write them on flash cards so that the students may practise them.

lower horizontal line. Finish your circle by going upwards to where you began and begin a straight line to the above horizontal line. Then make a straight line down to the bottom horizontal line through the line you already started." Write the numbers, 1, 2, and 3 in a different colored marker or chalk on one of the "a's" to show the steps. Then print another "a," quickly summarizing the method. Tell students to print an "a" in the air a few times or on individual chalk boards, if they have them. When they begin printing "a" in their books, have them whisper the steps to themselves in their own words. Ask them to print three or four of their best "a's." As they work, move from student to student checking pencil grip and the correct method of forming the letter. Make any corrections immediately.

The "a" example shows again how the whole-part-whole method of teaching may be used. Note, too, how printing is being taught using a multisensory approach incorporating oral, visual, and tactile senses.

Here are a few ways to help children remember how to print letters. Tack an alphabet at the front of the room with arrows that show how the letters are formed. Some students also benefit from having a copy of the alphabet taped to their desks. Others need as much practice printing the letters as possible, which can be done through classroom written work and commercially available photocopiable programs. Some children learn best by touching or manipulating things. Teach printing to these children by having them trace letters that are cut out of sandpaper and glued onto cardboard cards. To improve the way a child holds a pencil, attach a rubber pencil grip to the pencil so that the student learns how to hold it properly.

## Copying

If a child is slow copying notes from the board, there are three things you can do. You can reduce the amount of copying by providing a typed copy of the note in which key words are left blank. The child reads the note on the board and fills in the blanks on his paper. Alternatively, ask the child to copy as much as possible from the board, then provide a typed version of the note from which he may finish copying that evening. The third practice is to give extra time for copying. For example, if a note is assigned to be copied in the morning, let the child know that there will be time in the afternoon to finish the copying. Each of these techniques serves to reduce the anxiety a student feels when he knows that he can't finish the copying within the usual time limit.

## Written expression

Pre-writing activities can help students with their written expression. For example, if you want the children to write a story on a scary experience, then have a large-group discussion on people's experiences. Some children simply don't know what to write and discussing helps them to generate their own ideas. Write students' ideas and key words on the chalkboard or chart paper for reference. Before the children write their stories, direct them to develop an outline by completing a chart with the following headings: Introduction, Action, and Resolution (see page 58 for a sample; a reproducible version appears on page 122). They then write their points under each heading. As they write their stories, have them check off each section on their charts.

For editing, introduce the COPS method: **C**apitals, **O**verall appearance, **P**unctuation, and **S**pelling (Schumaker et al., 1981). You may use the form found on page 122 or write COPS on the board or on the inside cover of a child's notebook to serve as a reminder of what to look for when self-editing. Some students need to read their stories out loud to detect spelling errors and missing words or parts of sentences.

# Story Planner

Name: *Amanda (Gr. 6)*

Title: *The Soccer Tournament*

**Introduction** (Include where and when the story takes place, who the main characters are, and briefly what is happening.):

— *house league soccer practice, late summer, final tournament is next weekend*
— *Cathy, a forward, and Jen, the goalie, talk about everybody working on passing and shooting at the park after school*

**Action** (Describe the problem or conflict and how the main character handled it.):

— *Saturday Game 1 - played a team with really good players, never started passing - chasing the ball, lost 4:0*
— *Game 2 - won 3:2, passed in second half, Jen got two goals*
— *Game 3 - tired, played a weak team, Cathy made some good saves, Jen got all three goals by passing the ball*
— *Sunday Semis - played same team as in Game 2, Cathy made great saves, Jen helped on both goals, 2:1*
— *finals - same team as in Game 1, Jen scored just before the end of the first half, was tripped, sprained ankle, can't play, talks to team during half time, score at 1:0*
— *last two minutes player on other team gets a break away*

**Resolution** (Tell how the problem or conflict was resolved.):

— *Cathy jumped and made the save, they won the tournament*

For peer editing, match the struggling student with someone who is patient and has a solid understanding of spelling and grammar rules.

As far as producing a good copy goes, if a student has trouble writing the story, you may have to scribe it. Or, you may encourage older students to write their stories using a computer.

## Written assignments

Before the students begin working on an assignment, such as answering worksheet or textbook questions, it's wise to do the following: (1) Read the instructions to the class and orally summarize them; (2) discuss your expectations for answers, and if necessary, demonstrate on the board how to format answers. These two techniques help the students know what is to be done and how to do it.

Individual students may need special attention. Go to their desks and ask them to repeat the instructions back to you. Discuss the answer to the first question and ask the student you are focusing on to write it down. Place a check mark beside the question, assuming it is correct. This technique provides instant feedback and motivates the child to keep working. Discuss the answer to the next question and leave the student to answer it, returning later to check the answer. Then assign the next two or three questions and return to the student's desk within a specific time to monitor the work.

This technique, called *task analysis*, may also be applied to longer assignments. Basically, you divide the work into manageable chunks, check each section as it is completed, and provide immediate feedback. The technique effectively reduces the anxiety of doing a long assignment plus frequent checking provides opportunities for positive feedback, thus motivating the student.

When choosing a buddy to work with a child who has reading or writing difficulties, select a student who is capable and patient. Not all children are willing to help others by reading questions or discussing answers.

Other techniques can help students complete written assignments, too: reduce the number of questions (but not the quality of answers), give more time to do the assignment, and insist on seeing rough copies of projects which you can correct. To make projects look neater, encourage students to use a computer or an erasable pen. Alternatively, occasionally permit students to demonstrate their learning in ways other than writing, for example, through an oral presentation, dramatization, or a model.

## Mathematics

This section outlines techniques to help your students learn basic mathematical concepts and counting, arithmetic facts, operations, and problem solving. Before we move to those specific areas, though, here is a summary of fundamental techniques for teaching students who are experiencing general difficulties in math.

1. Let the children use manipulatives, for example, counters or an abacus for counting, or measuring tapes and containers to teach measurement.
2. For slower working children with difficulties in math, assign fewer questions if the concept is understood.
3. Review concepts, procedures, and facts frequently. Repetition is important to building long-term memory.
4. Tape a number line to an individual student's desk and have him use it by touching the numbers as he counts.

5. Teach the procedures for adding, subtracting, multiplying, and dividing by demonstrating each step. Write the procedures on chart paper posted in the classroom to remind students of the steps.
6. Help students, especially older ones who may never know all of the arithmetic facts, by providing fact tables and permitting the use of calculators.
7. Distribute graph paper or notebooks formatted in graph paper to help those students who have difficulty aligning columns of numbers.
8. If a student has difficulty with copying (e.g., reversing numbers), give her a photocopy of the assignment to eliminate problems in copying the questions.
9. Pair a child with a buddy who can read directions and word problems and answer quick questions about the work.
10. Teach estimation so that the student may assess whether her final answer is remotely correct.

*Counting:* Use a *multisensory* method to teach students how to count. Post a number line at the front of the classroom and on the student's desk so that she may see the numbers. Orally count with the child so that she hears the numbers. Have the child point to the numbers as they are being said to establish a relationship between what is said and what is seen. Use manipulatives to teach counting so that the student may touch the objects when counting and put them into groups, such as five of something.

Repetition is important when working with children who experience difficulty in counting. Therefore, provide as many opportunities to count in the classroom as possible. Finally, encourage students to play board games that involve counting, such as Snakes and Ladders, and software that reinforces counting.

*Mathematical Facts:* Many children who have difficulty remembering their facts benefit from a multisensory approach and much repetition. To teach facts effectively, have the children touch manipulatives so that they can understand that $3 - 2 = 1$, for example. Have them say the math fact so that they hear it and write it so that they see it. Older students may want to use a number line which they touch with their index finger when answering questions involving addition and subtraction facts.

Use the principle of going from the known to the unknown when teaching multiplication and division facts. Teach multiplication as addition, for example, $3 + 3 + 3 + 3 = 12$ or $3 \times 4 = 12$. Teach division as subtraction, for example, 8 take away 2 four times gives us four groups of two, or $8 \div 2 = 4$. Let the children work with counters to reinforce the concepts.

For students who have difficulty remembering the facts, provide opportunities for review. Students could work with partners using flash cards. Setting aside the first five minutes of each math period for review is another option. After you write five to 10 fact questions on the board, direct the students to copy them into their notebooks and answer them. Then take up the answers by writing the correct numbers on the board and asking children to check their own work. You could also distribute a sheet of various math facts and see how many questions students can answer in one minute. Once the sheets are corrected, let students graph their own progress using the inside back cover of their notebooks. A good idea is to have students make special folders in which to place the sheets they accumulate.

*Operations (adding, subtracting, multiplying, and dividing):* Teach each procedure in a step-by-step manner. Use chart paper to show an example and number each step beside the spot in the calculation where it is shown. Use a different colored marker for labeling steps. Direct the children to copy the example into their notes with the steps labeled; it will later serve as a guide when they're working independently. Next, write three practice questions on the board and ask the students to do them at their desks. Then correct the work together and review the procedures. The final step is independent practice whereby the students answer questions on their own. At the end of the lesson, post the chart paper in the classroom as a reference for students.

Encourage any students who have difficulty remembering the steps to the operation to whisper the steps to themselves and to use counters for some of the adding or subtracting. The multisensory approach helps a student receive the message from a variety of learning channels (auditory, visual, and tactile). Also, during the seatwork period, check the work of any student who frequently finds it hard to remember to ensure that the student understands the procedures and can do the work correctly. Place check marks beside correct answers to give instant positive feedback.

*Problem Solving:* When instructing students on problem solving, teach the words and phrases that alert them to specific operations and post them in the classroom.

1. Multiply and carry.
2. Multiply.
3. Add the number that was carried.

- *how many*, *total number* (adding or multiplying)
  Examples: How many points do the boys have? What is the total amount of the bill?
- *how many more*, *how many fewer*, *how many are left* (subtracting)
  Examples: How many more slices of pizza are in the large size than the small size? How many fewer toy cars does Shelly have than Amanda? When Dylan takes away his cards, how many are left?
- *how many does each have* (dividing)
  Example: If the candies are divided equally among the students, how many does each have?

Drawing diagrams for problems involving perimeter and area works well. Also, if big numbers confuse a student, suggest that she substitute smaller numbers (e.g., from 1 to 10) to figure out which operation to use, then solve the problem.

Some ways to help students who are having difficulty with problem solving include underlining key words, having someone read the problem aloud, and making up problems that have some relevance to a student's life. Teach a viable method for solving problems, such as *read*, *think*, *draw*, *solve*, and *write*. (Page 68 outlines a variation.) This method serves as a good way of demonstrating problem solving to individuals or the entire class.

**Listening and following directions**

Before you begin teaching, ensure that students are listening to you.

- Tell all of the children to put away their materials and listen. You might reinforce this by having a traffic light made of construction paper posted on the board. A magnetic arrow pointed to the red circle will reinforce no talking.

For younger students, limit the time you spend presenting material to less than 10 minutes. Changing activities every 10 minutes is another option.

- For the child who is finding it hard to listen, make eye contact, seat him close to you, use a special cue, or say the student's name quietly. Ensure that all distracting material is off the desk.

During the lesson, involve the struggling listener as much as possible through question and answer or by helping you demonstrate something. Shorten the length of your presentations to prevent loss of focus by distractable students, and vary the activities in your lessons (e.g., teacher-centred, small-group, and large-group activities).

When giving instructions for an assignment, use plenty of visual support: hold up the textbook at the correct page or hold up the worksheet, write the page number on the board, note the instructions on paper or on the board, and demonstrate what you want done. For instructions printed in the book or on the sheet, provide the class with paraphrases in simple language. You might have a student repeat the instructions back to you individually. Some students also benefit by having a written copy of the numbered instructions, which can be checked off as they are met.

### Remembering

There are four ways you can help students remember what they have been taught: by motivating them, taking a multisensory approach, using mnemonic devices, and providing *lots* of repetition. To motivate students, let them know what will be studied and why and show them how this new information relates to their own lives. Write the name of the topic on the board. Teach from the known to the unknown by asking the students questions that demand recall. The question-and-answer technique involves them immediately in the lesson and helps them remember information that will be helpful in learning the new concept.

Here's another example of a mnemonic device. This one would help students remember the lines of a musical staff, E, G, B, D, F: Every Good Boy Deserves a Ferrari.

When teaching the new concept, use as much visual and tactile support for your words as possible. Using a multisensory approach helps all students receive the message through three different channels, one of which should prove to be a strength. Involve a student as much as possible in the presentation of the concept through questions or demonstration of points. While teaching, present ways for students to remember the points through mnemonic devices, for example, the acronym HOMES for the great lakes (**H**uron, **O**ntario, **M**ichigan, **E**rie, and **S**uperior). Encourage the students to think of their own ways of remembering facts. Some children like to make up songs to help them remember lists of things.

After teaching the lesson, provide opportunities for review through repetition. For example, in the "pair share" technique, pairs of students take two to three minutes to tell each other what they have just learned. As well, you might provide students with books taken out from the school library on the topic and have software available for review of material. You could also begin future lessons by reviewing previously learned concepts on a topic.

### Organization

The most important thing you can do to help a student who is disorganized is to provide a very organized environment. Here are some things you can do to make it possible for the student to help herself.

- ✔ Punch all handouts and give class time (30 to 60 seconds) to permit students to insert them into their binders. Provide five minutes for any handouts you want glued. If you *don't* give class time, then the papers will not be in the notebooks.

✔ Check the student's notebook often to ensure that it is complete. If not, photocopy notes from other students and have her copy or insert them.

✔ Pair each student with a "study buddy" who may be telephoned during an absence to get the homework.

✔ Have a model notebook available so that students can organize their notes following the pattern and photocopy any notes that they are missing.

✔ When a class assignment has been given, go to the student's desk. Discuss the first question and either watch her write the answer or return to check it. Provide positive feedback after you check the answer.

✔ For longer or out-of-class assignments, type all instructions and evaluation criteria, distribute them to students, and have parents sign the page (up to junior high). Give marks for each segment of the project, including the outline, the rough draft, and the final draft. This technique helps you to monitor student progress and give feedback.

The student with poor organizational skills may also have one set of textbooks and a pencil case for school and another for home. Adopting this practice overcomes the problem of forgetting things. For older students, the collateral approach works well. As mentioned earlier, if a student forgets a pen, lend him one with collateral, such as a shoe. At the end of the class, exchange items.

Having a designated place for classroom materials promotes better organization. Younger students can place all of their materials in a large plastic tub stored under their desks. This practice helps keep a child's things confined to one area. Older students can color-code their textbooks and binders to help them bring the correct ones to class. Sometimes, students find it easier to carry one binder for the morning subjects and another one for afternoon classes.

It is sometimes helpful for older students to organize their looseleaf notebooks with a table of contents and page numbers. It also allows you to see what notes are missing just by looking at the contents. You can aid organization further by photocopying review sheets on colored paper and tests on buff, which helps to identify the beginning and ending of units in the notebook. Prompt the students to study for final exams from the colored sheets at the end of each unit.

Help students know the class schedule too. For non-rotary classes, post the weekly schedule so that the children can see it. Older students should have copies of personal timetables in their lockers, pencil cases, and binders, and at home. Having quick access to the schedule helps students know where to be when. As well, at the beginning of each lesson, write an agenda on the board and review it. The agenda reduces anxiety about what activities will be done in a period and helps students mentally prepare for the work.

You can take concrete measures to help students overcome difficulties in organizing their homework. At the end of the day or class period, take five minutes to list the homework and information on projects and tests on the Homework section of the board. Direct the students to copy the information into their planners or agendas. You may have to sign some agendas in order to indicate to parents that all the homework is recorded. Give younger students a minute or two before the final bell to place homework in their knapsacks. Some students may need a buddy to check off the homework as it is placed in the knapsack. Providing class time for students to organize their homework helps them to get it home and sends a message that you are serious about it.

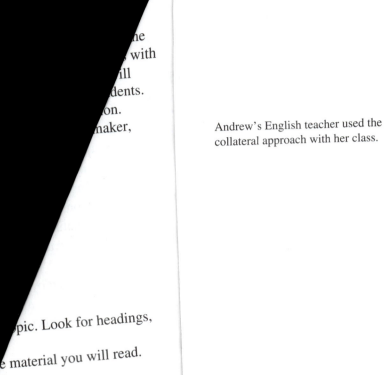

Andrew's English teacher used the collateral approach with her class.

Using written agendas with *all* students who can read is a good idea. The agenda also helps to keep *you* on track! As for non-readers, simply tell them what you will be doing.

he
with
ill
dents.
on.
naker,

pic. Look for headings,

e material you will read.
ed.
f questions about the section you
write point-form notes.
ding the material and making notes,

the process of making sense of words
read and making notes about the key

kills
unger students also help junior high and
dent deal with everyday spelling, permit use
or electronic spelling device. For out-of-clas
t to type assignments, using the spell-check
a student's handwriting is poor, encourage h
to space out the letters so that you can read
dents to use a laptop computer in the classro
of in-class assignments. For students with ve
miting the amount of marks deducted for spe

isplayed

65

# What to Look for in Students Suspected of Having a Learning Disability

## JUNIOR HIGH AND HIGH SCHOOL STUDENTS

**Basic Reading Skills and Reading Comprehension**
- ❑ lacks fluency, accuracy, speed
- ❑ loses place, skips words or lines
- ❑ repeats words
- ❑ shows discrepancy between oral and silent reading
- ❑ confuses similar letters, words, sounds
- ❑ follows with a finger, ruler, or pencil
- ❑ unwilling to read aloud
- ❑ has difficulty finding main idea and in making

**Spelling**
- ❑ spells the same words in the same pass
- ❑ reverses letters
- ❑ faces difficulty in associating sou
- ❑ puts letters in words in incorrec
- ❑ omits last letters, capitals

**Writing Skills and Written**
- ❑ handwrites illegibly
- ❑ shows inability to
- ❑ handwrites slov
- ❑ writes and pr
- ❑ omits date
- ❑ poor se
- ❑ what is
- ❑ doesn't con

**Oral Skills**
- ❑ speaks hesitantly
- ❑ forgets common words
- ❑ has poor grammar compared
- ❑ generally poor verbal expression
- ❑ avoids oral participation and discussi

**Listening**
- ❑ misunderstands ideas and directions presented o
- ❑ remembers information poorly
- ❑ has difficulty sequencing instructions
- ❑ confuses similar sounds
- ❑ takes no notes or poor notes from oral presentations

© 2001 Students at Risk by Cheryll Duquette. Pembroke Publishers Limited. All rights reserved. Permission to reproduce for clas

---

## Ways to Help Junior High and High School Students Learn

### Reading skills

*Novels, Plays, and Short Stories*: In English class, effective pre-reading activities include discussing new vocabulary words and personal experiences that relate to the plot. Read the novel, play, or short story to gain a general understanding of the plot. Read the novel, play, or short story to the students during class time or provide an audiotape to take home. Encourage the students to visualize the action and characters and discuss the elements of the story with the class. To further enhance comprehension, dramatize scenes from the story.

*Text in Content Areas*: To improve comprehension of printed text, provide students with a copy of new vocabulary with definitions. Discuss the terms with the class. As well, try to find textbooks with pictures and diagrams that will break up the written sections. Too much print may overwhelm some students. Look for subheadings and margin notes that help summarize information. The following two strategies, RAP paraphrasing and SQR3 (Schul, Deshler, Alley, & Denton, 1982), will help students improve their comprehension of text.

*RAP Paraphrasing*
- **R**ead one or two paragraphs.
- **A**sk yourself what you just read.
- **P**ut it into your own words.
- Write jot notes, if necessary.

*SQR3*
- **S**urvey — Skim material to get an idea of the t subheadings, and words in boldface.
- **Q**uestion — Ask yourself questions about th
- **R**ead — Answer the questions you just ask
- **R**ecite — Cover the book and ask yourse just read. Some people find it helpful to
- **R**eview — When you have finished re review the passage and notes.

Both methods actively engage readers by having them question what was in ideas.

Older students still enjoy being read to, and benefit from the practice. Sometimes, audiotapes of the story are available; however, you usually have to make them yourself. Reading individually with an audiotape speeds up the reading process, improves comprehension, and increases attention span.

### Spelling, grammar, handwo

Some accommodations us high school students If of a spelling dicti and assignments e stu and gramm lity to write ler li Yo

With older students, the focus is less on remediation and more on teaching coping skills. It is believed that once a student is beyond Grade 6, more of the same kinds of remediation activities will not make much of a difference in performance. Therefore, the student is taught how to work around specific weaknesses.

Andrew's English teacher used many of these ideas with him.

## Written assignments

As you plan the assignment, consider dividing it up into stages of work, such as planning, draft, and final copy. Give marks for each stage. Doing this enables you to keep track of each student's progress and motivate students. When you introduce a big assignment to your students, it's best to distribute a typewritten sheet with instructions that specify exactly what is to be done when, the assessment criteria, and mark weightings. Read the instructions to them. Having junior high students' parents sign the sheet ensures that they are aware of the assignment.

Before the students begin work, discuss ideas for the assignment with the entire class or with specific students. Demonstrate exactly what you want done and provide an example of a completed assignment, if possible. If your students need to know, teach them how to research a topic using the library and the Internet. (A resource such as *Information Transformation* by Tricia Armstrong, published in 2000 by Pembroke, may help you.) As well, develop a form that will help students organize their information on a topic into headings which will later become sections in a report. Teaching students how to write a five-paragraph essay expressing a point of view may also help them. (See page 27 to see how Andrew's teacher did this.)

Some students may require extra time to complete the assignment. As one student with a learning disability told me, an extra day can make a big difference in the quality of the work. When it comes to negotiating an extension, be clear that the student must approach you *before* the due date, and that the two of you will decide on a new date. Announce your policy to the class before the assignments are under way. When the students are at the editing stage, provide consultation to improve content, expression, and mechanics. Finally, consider permitting a student who has great difficulty completing written work to do part of the assignment in oral form. Some people can express what they know much better orally than on paper.

## Mathematics

It's important to introduce a new concept or procedure systematically. First, write the title on the board or acetate. Review what has previously been learned to help the students feel confident about beginning something new and to contextualize the new material. Work through an example on the board, showing *all* the steps and numbering them preferably in colored chalk. After completing your example, verbally summarize the procedure while pointing to the steps. Direct students to do two or three examples in their notebooks. Take up the answers on the board and repeat the procedures, while students make any necessary corrections. Then assign them the work, stating the page number and writing it on the board, as well as all of the questions to be answered. Be sure to discuss how to solve the more difficult questions. While the students are working, move from desk to desk monitoring and assisting.

Some students will require accommodations in math. A number of them will not know their facts (and may *never* know them all) so permit them to use a calculator. When teaching integers, encourage students to refer to a number line and to use their index finger to count the numbers. Also, some students may have difficulty aligning numbers in columns: ask them to bring a notebook entirely of graph paper. Consider permitting students to work in pairs so that math concepts may be discussed. Partner a weaker student with one who is patient and who understands the concepts. You should also provide as much

Andrew's English teacher used the procedure for extensions and gave him some opportunities to present orally with positive results.

one-to-one assistance as possible and have regularly scheduled extra help sessions for all students.

---

**Mathematical Problem Solving**

Here is a logical, five-step approach you can introduce to students who experience difficulty with problem solving.

1. Read the problem and underline key words.
2. Think about what information you know and what you have to find out.
3. Draw a sketch to show the information. If you find big numbers difficult to understand, mentally replace the big ones with small numbers to help you decide what operations are necessary.
4. Estimate what the answer should be.
5. Solve the problem and compare it to your estimation.

---

When correcting daily work, ensure that the answers are said aloud and written on the board. Doing this accommodates the needs of both auditory and visual learners. For longer solutions, have the students write them on the board. As you correct them, review the steps that were followed. Insist that *all* mistakes be corrected to ensure that the notebook is a record of accurate answers.

When scheduling a test, provide as much warning as possible so that students may study. Teach the students how to study for math: do sample questions and check them with the answers in your notebook. You may want to permit students to bring a "cheat sheet" to a test. In this case, specify the desired size of paper and which formulas should be on it. The day before the test, the students should bring their sheets to class for you to initial.

The period before the test, you could give the students a review sheet formatted similarly to the test. Doing the review sheet helps some students with difficulties in math to feel confident about the test. It may also be the only studying a student does. Correct the review sheet and repeat the steps in the procedures for solving questions.

Once students write the test, return it as promptly as possible to provide feedback. Correct the answers to the test together on the board and ensure that students make necessary corrections. It's recommended that students in junior high have all tests signed by a parent.

### Copying and note taking

Give students who are slow in copying notes from the board or acetates a copy of your notes so that they don't have to look up from their work, find the correct spot, and look down again. You may also consider providing students with a fill-in-the-blank version of the notes. They would then have to copy only key words from the board onto their sheets.

When you plan to show a video, take advantage of the start/stop features of the technology. Distribute a viewing guide sheet with questions and spaces for the students to write their answers. You might put the tape on pause as each question is answered, discuss the answer with the class, and give students a few minutes to write the answer on their sheet. If you don't want to pause the video, take up the answers at the end of the video and insist that students correct their work and include all information.

If you use the lecture method, plan to provide visual support for students whose learning strength is through the visual channel. For these students, write key ideas on an acetate or the board, distribute an organizer with headings, subheadings, and spaces to write point-form notes, teach the students how to make notes, and encourage them to develop their own abbreviations for words. Cue students about key points by saying, "This point is important." Write such points on the board and repeat them. For students who are unable to listen and copy at the same time, provide a photocopy of your lecture notes or permit them to bring a cassette tape recorder to class. Students who have poor handwriting or a poor memory should be encouraged to type their lecture notes that evening. Adopting this practice ensures that the notes are in a readable form and provides an opportunity for the students to review their notes.

## Create an Enabling Environment

By now, you should better understand learning disabilities, their characteristics, and ideas for accommodation. These classroom suggestions may be used with students who have been identified as having a learning disability *and* with those students who have not been identified, but show weaknesses in specific areas, such as reading or copying.

When planning lessons, remember the four teaching methods described in this chapter: multisensory, moving from the known to the unknown, whole-part-whole, and task analysis. They will assist *all* children to understand better the concepts you are teaching. Also, remember to demonstrate what you want done in an assignment and review procedures, concepts, and facts often. Repetition is important.

Your goal is to create an environment in which students, including any with learning disabilities, can enjoy success. To do this, you have to know the students' strengths and weaknesses. You also have to be organized and patient.

Will every child with a learning disability succeed in an enabling environment? Success will depend on three elements: your willingness to make accommodations, the student's willingness to keep trying and to engage in the activities you have planned, and the involvement of the parents. All three are needed to make progress. However, for success to begin to happen, you must take the initial steps. By reading this book, you are further on your way to providing an environment in which all students can experience success.

When lecturing, consider photocopying the paper copy of your acetate for students who have difficulty taking notes.

The same basic ideas on listening and following directions, remembering, and organization apply to both elementary and junior high/high school students. See pages 61–63.

# CHAPTER 6

# Behavioral Disorders

In this chapter you will learn how to work effectively with students who act-out, behave in a withdrawn manner, or who have been diagnosed as having AD/HD.

## Acting-out Behaviors

We all know the frustration of working with students who exhibit acting-out behaviors. They not only challenge our authority and disrupt the classroom, but they also take valuable learning time away from the well-behaved students. Although most people want to be liked and accepted by others, some choose inappropriate ways to try to achieve this goal. Dreikurs and Cassel (1992) suggest that children misbehave for the following reasons:

- to gain attention
- to seek power
- to exact retribution or revenge for real or perceived injustices
- to conceal a feeling of inadequacy

*Attention Seeking:* If you suspect that a student is misbehaving to seek attention, try not to give attention if it's a minor inappropriate behavior, such as excessive pencil sharpening, finger tapping, or playing with a toy. Instead, use *proximity control* and move towards the child. Standing close to the student usually causes the inappropriate behavior to stop. You may also have to say the student's name in a quiet voice. Your behaviors send a message to the student to stop the inappropriate behavior without giving her attention for misbehaving. On the other hand, give attention to the student for positive behaviors, such as bringing learning materials to class, sitting properly, and not pushing in line. Doing so reinforces the desirable behaviors. With older students, state praise in a quiet voice to avoid embarrassment.

*Power Seeking:* Sometimes, the student misbehaves as a way of seeking power. Knowing this, try not to argue with the student. This is what she wants. Rather, use the *broken record* technique: state the expected behavior, such as "In our class we sit on our chairs," in a positive way and use a calm, firm voice. Move close to the student and be sure to look her in the eye as you repeat the

Calmness is strength. Remember not to show annoyance and to remain firm, but fair.

statement of expected behavior. And remember, you don't have to have the last word in a discussion.

One way to deal with the power issue is to share it. Offer *choices* to the student, for example, "You may do this assignment now, or you may do it for homework" or "This is the work that has to be done; you may do it in any order."

You can also present *logical consequences* for behaving a certain way. Have a few clearly defined rules which you enforce at all times, such as no talking during a test. If a student breaks one of the rules, state the rule and the consequences, then offer a choice of action. For example, if you notice that two students are whispering to one another during a test, walk over to their desks and quietly remind them of the rule and the consequences if it's broken. You might say something like this: "During the test there is no talking. If you choose to talk anymore during this test, then you will each receive a zero. The choice is yours." If they force you to invoke the consequences, their quarrel is with the rules and not you.

Below are some typical classroom misbehaviors that violate rules and their consequences.

*Elementary Level*

- Excessive talking that is unrelated to the work: Work alone at another desk or seat.
- Touching others during circle time: Move away from others.
- Pushing in line: Move to the back of the line.
- Not completing work: Take it home for homework with a note written in the agenda.
- Playing with a toy during instruction: Place toy inside the desk, or place toy on the teacher's desk to be returned at recess.

*Junior High and High School Level*

- Late or nonsubmission of assignments: Marks will be lost.
- Late to class: Have a detention at the office (as a school rule) or make up the missed time after class.
- Excessive talking: Move to another seat or work alone.
- Fighting or swearing: Go to the office (a school rule).

*Revenge Seeking:* Yes, you may encounter a student who seeks revenge on you for whatever reason. Although you may feel hurt by the student's meanness, try not to reveal your vulnerability. As hard at it may be, find something positive about the student and use it constructively in class; for example, an interest in science may be applied to a variety of subject areas. Try to develop a positive relationship with the student by talking with him or her about personal interests too.

Do your best to show that you like the student, but not the disturbing behavior. You may say, "Jennifer, I like you, but when you talk while I'm giving instructions, it makes it difficult for the others to hear. And Jennifer, they don't know what to do. You're not being fair to them. I would like you to listen when instructions are given." And when Jennifer is silent or behaves appropriately, offer praise. You could quietly make a comment or write something positive in the margin of an assignment.

If you state the rules, describe consequences, and give choices, you are unlikely to feel guilty about administering consequences. You'll be able to administer them in a calm way because it is clear to others in the classroom that a student has chosen to break a known rule. The subjective element is gone.

Don't give students any openings to think about revenge. Being polite to all students and never centring anyone out blunts any student's inclination to seek revenge. It's especially effective to treat older students in this way. However, once a teacher has yelled at a student in class, the student may decide he has the perfect reason to "get back" at the teacher. Reminding students of the rules, stating consequences, offering choices, and showing respect for your students will eliminate rationalizations for revenge.

*Feelings of Inadequacy:* A student prone to such feelings may misbehave in order to get out of doing work or to delay starting work which he doubts he can complete successfully.

What is needed here is much encouragement and praise. Plan activities in which you know the child can be successful. For example, let the child help you when you are teaching or demonstrate a skill, perhaps in the arts.

Another useful technique is *task analysis.* Break the work down into smaller components, give a short time limit to complete each segment, help the child get started, leave, return after the allotted time, correct the work that is done, and offer praise. Assign another section of work, leave, and return. Repeat this process and gradually increase the length of time between visits. This technique is also valuable with students who have learned helplessness and who want you to do the work for them.

## Twenty-five Ways to Minimize Behavior Problems in Your Classroom

Establishing a positive relationship with your students is likely the most effective strategy that you can use to promote desirable behavior in your classroom. All students want to feel that they are liked by the teacher and that this adult can be trusted not to make them look bad in front of others. This isn't to say that social relations should be the goal of your work in the classroom. A positive and trusting relationship is the basis for the work of the classroom: teaching and learning.

The second best way to foster good behavior is through lesson planning and preparation. Develop interesting lessons and incorporate activities in which the students can be successful. As well, have all of your materials ready for use so that there are no "dead" spots in the delivery.

Below are more ideas to help reduce behavior problems in the classroom.

1. Model respectful behavior. When asking a student to do something, use the words "please" and "thank you." Always speak positively of others and treat others the way you want to be treated. Once you have established a tone of respect, the students will follow your lead.
2. Know the students' strengths, weaknesses, and situations that trigger an outburst.
3. Help the students feel good about themselves. Convey the idea that you like them, but not the problem behavior.
4. Focus on success in academic areas, including sports and the arts.
5. Provide students with opportunities to make choices (e.g., if you speak politely and respectfully, you may work with this group, or you may complete the assignment alone at your own desk).

Alex's teacher (see Chapter 4) recognized Alex's skill in swimming and posted a newspaper article about it.

Andrew, who was asked to tally how many times he missed or came late to class, was amazed to discover how often he thought of skipping (see Chapter 4).

6. Develop a few classroom rules, for example, respect yourself and your property, and respect other people and their property. Establish logical consequences for misbehavior and enforce them *consistently*.

7. Pinpoint and analyze a student's misbehavior (e.g., hitting others, wandering in the classroom). Make observations of the student through tally counts to determine frequency and duration. Use these data to hypothesize reasons for inappropriate behavior and to make a plan to change the behavior. For example, you may notice that a student talks to others and wanders around the classroom to avoid tasks that he or she does not enjoy. You may then decide to provide some one-to-one attention to that child when doing those tasks: reviewing requirements, helping him or her get started on the work, checking questions frequently and providing feedback.

8. Involve students in monitoring their own behavior (*self-monitoring*). Pinpoint a specific behavior, for example, calling out answers. On a sheet of paper, have the student do a tally count each time he or she engages in that behavior. You should also try to keep track of the behavior using the same system. At the end of class or an agreed-upon time frame, discuss your observations with the student. This method helps to make the student aware of the frequency of the behavior, which may lead to a decrease in it. You may also want to reward the student for having correctly counted the number of infractions, that is to say, your totals match. Self-monitoring might also be used as part of a reward program for the student.

9. Closely supervise the students to ensure that misbehavior does not occur. Consider being in your classroom at all times to ensure that incidents do not happen.

10. Observe the student who is having a tantrum or outburst to determine the triggers that may have caused it, the actual behavior, and the aftermath. As mentioned previously, follow the ABC method (A = antecedents, B = behavior — duration and frequency, and C = consequences). For example, a student may feel overwhelmed by two chalkboards of writing to be copied, show signs of frustration, then overturn his desk and storm out of the classroom. Once you know that copying is difficult for the child, you may either give the student a sheet on which the note is typed but the student has to insert key words in the blanks or ask the student to copy as much as possible and later provide a photocopy.

11. Adhere closely to routines and the class schedule. They provide security and a predictable environment for the students. Write the agenda and the homework on the chalkboard in the same spot each day. If variations to the schedule emerge, explain them to the students ahead of time.

12. If you find yourself in an argument with a student, move to a location where you can speak to that student alone. A hallway may suffice. Remain calm and lower your voice. Try to de-escalate the conflict. Whenever possible, allow the student to "save face."

13. Some students may need to have opportunities for physical movement built into an activity. For some students getting out of their seats and placing completed work in the In box is all that is required. Others need to manipulate objects in math and science. Another possibility is to organize your lesson so that the students meet in small groups, which involves getting out of the desk, or in centres to which the students rotate every 10 to 15 minutes.

Using I-messages helped Alex's teacher remain calm, and nonverbal cuing helped Alex stay on-task (see Chapter 4).

14. Use I-messages (Gordon, 1974). "I am disturbed when you throw your pencil in the class because it may injure other students. I want you to keep your pencil in your hand or in your pencil case." Be sure to speak calmly and firmly.

15. Use nonverbal cuing and proximity to correct minor misbehavior. For example, to remind a student to be quiet, place your index finger at right angles to your lips. Most students will respond and engage in appropriate behavior.

16. Provide as much genuine feedback as possible. Try to use words that praise the student's work, such as "I like the way you have shown all your work when answering this math question." Positive feedback helps to shape appropriate behaviors because students know what you want. Negative feedback only tells them what you don't want, and they have to guess at what you want. It's simple: tell them what behavior you expect *before* the event happens or the work is assigned and praise them for doing the appropriate thing.

17. Make students accountable for their actions. Beyond using proximity control (moving near the student whose behavior is disruptive to the functioning of the class) and nonverbal cuing, do the following.

---

### How to Make Students Accountable for Their Actions

Behavior: Talking while you are instructing the class

- State the student's name and the behavior expected. For example: "Nicole, I would like you to stop talking so that the others have the opportunity to learn." Say this in a firm, but non-threatening tone of voice. Usually, the student will stop talking.
- If the student continues to talk, offer her a choice: "Nicole, you may sit where you are and not talk or take a seat at the back of the classroom away from the others." She will likely stop talking, or she may take a seat at the back with some bravado.
- If she continues to talk in either location, firmly say, "You have chosen to continue to talk. You will have to leave the room and go to the office." The student will likely leave in a huff. Contact the office and tell the staff that she should be expected. Resume teaching.
- After class, find out what happened at the office. During or immediately after the next class, talk to the student privately. Ask her why she misbehaved and how she will change her behavior.

Note that in this case, Nicole is aware of the expected behavior and is making choices as to how she is going to behave. At all times, remain firm, but non-threatening and calm. You are just enforcing rules and consequences. You are not punishing the student, but rather she is choosing to disrupt the class, and known consequences apply. If she decides to comply at any point, privately acknowledge her behavior.

---

18. Watch for signs of frustration in students. By intervening when you observe that a student is becoming frustrated, you may be able to defuse a potentially explosive situation. Johns and Carr (1995) describe four stages of frustration; appropriate responses are also outlined.

1) *Anxiety stage:* The student shows nonverbal signs, such as sighs and putting his or her head down. Respond by listening actively and talking in a non-judgmental fashion.

2) *Stress stage:* The student often shows frustration through minor behavior problems, such as tearing paper or tapping a pencil. Use proximity control to redirect behavior or boost the child's interest and motivation by providing assistance with the assignment.

3) *Physical stage:* The student has lost control and begins to threaten others, throw objects, or hit others. Remind the student that he or she still has choices, escort the student from class, get help from other staff, protect the safety of the other students, and restrain the student if necessary.

4) *Tension reduction stage:* The student releases tension through crying or verbal venting. Show empathy and help the student gain insight into his or her feelings and behavior.

Students may be confused and frightened by their lack of self-control during stressful situations. They are often receptive to those who respect their dignity while providing assistance.

19. A teacher's response to a particular behavior can escalate or de-escalate the problem. If you react by presenting an ultimatum, the student may take the challenge (e.g., don't say another word or I'll throw you out of class). Colvin, Ainge, and Nelson (1997) recommend that when a student displays defiant, challenging, or inappropriate behavior the teacher do three things:

1) State the rule or expectation.

2) Request explicitly for the student to "take care of the problem."

3) Present options for the student on how to take care of the problem. This course of action provides a way for the student to back down and save face in front of peers.

20. Train yourself to cue students to demonstrate the correct behavior. For example, during a large-group discussion when the students are talking out of turn, you could do the following:

- Decide exactly what behaviors you want to see, such as raising their hands and waiting to be called upon.
- Tell the students what behavior you want to see. For example, say, "Raise your hand if you want to speak and I'll do my best to call on you" or "I'll only call on those people who choose to raise their hands."
- Phrase your questions as follows: "Raise your hand if you can tell us . . . " This phrase cues students to raise their hands and tells them that you are serious about having them do it.
- Call on *only* those students who raise their hands.

21. Involve the students as much as possible during a lesson through questioning, doing board work, or hands-on activities. Learning is enhanced and off-task behaviors minimized.

22. Use task analysis, where you break down the task into smaller units and ensure that each segment is completed to the required standard. For example, if there are 20 math questions, direct the student to do five at a time and check each group of five as they are completed. Provide positive feedback as each set of five questions is corrected. Breaking a large task into chunks that the student can accomplish makes it seem more manageable. For certain assignments, marks can be given for the completion of each

Alex's teacher found that it was far more constructive to monitor the girl for signs of agitation and intervene early than to wait till yelling became "necessary."

Alex's teacher came to realize that her own inconsistent following of the hands-up rule may have contributed to Alex's tendency to speak out of turn.

Task analysis, coupled with a system of rewards, enabled Alex to complete longer assignments successfully.

segment. This technique helps motivate the child to stay on-task instead of trying to avoid it because it looks too daunting.

23. Give precise instructions. Using simple words, tell the students exactly what has to be done and demonstrate how to do it. Ask specific students to repeat the instructions back to you. As well, state the expectations for quality of work and behavior while working on the assignment. This technique eliminates guessing at what is to be done and what you consider to be appropriate behavior.

24. Provide *meaningful* activities for "fast finishers" or those who require enrichment (see Chapter 9 for more ideas). Such activities extend the skill or concept so that the student can explore the topic further or deeply. Give students opportunities to earn marks for successful completion of enrichment assignments.

25. Look beyond the behaviors a student is exhibiting to consider whether an underlying problem is not being addressed. For example, a student who doesn't seem to pay attention to oral instructions may have a mild hearing impairment or a learning disability involving the processing of oral language.

One reason that Erik's homeroom and music teachers wanted to provide him with enrichment activities was to avoid the development of behavior problems (see Chapter 3).

In Andrew's case, the behavior problems stemmed from the student's feeling he could not do the written English work (see Chapter 2).

---

**Classroom Behavior Taboos for Teachers**

Remember: You always want to serve as a positive model for your students. If your behavior isn't up to par, you can't expect theirs to be.

- Never nag. Students stop listening to you.
- Don't issue threats or ultimatums. You usually don't have the power to carry them out.
- Avoid making hasty judgments and acting without thought. Take time to calm down before you speak to a student whose actions disturb you or the class.
- Don't overreact to minor incidents.
- Avoid arbitrary or inconsistent enforcement of the rules.
- Don't yell, scream, or even talk very loudly.
- Do not implement inappropriate or harsh punishments. You will set yourself up as a target for revenge.

---

## Withdrawn Behavior

While some students may act-out in your class, others may internalize their problems. It is easy to overlook those who are excessively withdrawn because they are so undemanding of your time. However, they also need your attention. Page 77 outlines typical behaviors.

## How to Help Withdrawn Students

Develop a positive relationship with such students. First, strive to establish a personal rapport. Smile at the student and say "Hello," then engage the student in light conversation about sports, news events, school activities, or anything the student may enjoy. Striking a conversation may be difficult initially, but persist.

# Some Behaviors of Students Who Are Excessively Shy and Withdrawn

No child who is withdrawn will show all of the behaviors listed below. Look for those behaviors that are shown *frequently over time*.

- ❑ rarely contributes to class discussions

- ❑ rarely asks for assistance

- ❑ arrives late for class

- ❑ does not come to school

- ❑ appears anxious, nervous, or fearful

- ❑ may cry easily when confronted by you or student peers

- ❑ lingers in the classroom to avoid social situations

- ❑ walks close to the hallway walls with head down to avoid social contact

- ❑ plays alone, eats lunch alone, walks home alone, or sits alone on the bus

- ❑ complains of headaches or of feeling sick to avoid school and social interaction

- ❑ may have nightmares and poor sleeping habits

- ❑ may engage in self-abusive behaviors

Second, try to provide opportunities for success in the classroom. From an academic perspective, this may be done by giving individual assistance and by asking the student to demonstrate a skill that he has mastered or to explain what you know to be a correct answer to the class. In each of these situations, provide quiet praise.

To help the student feel comfortable in groups, begin with pairs. Larger groups might be too intimidating to a withdrawn student. Match the student with another student of the same sex who is easygoing and tolerant. Have them work on a task that you know the withdrawn student can do well and will enjoy. Gradually move up to larger groups. Privately praise the withdrawn student for participating and for the completed work.

Both of these techniques help the withdrawn student feel comfortable with you and the other students in the classroom. Providing opportunities for academic success and positive feedback increases the student's comfort level and the possibility of the student becoming less withdrawn.

## Attention Deficit/Hyperactivity Disorder

Students with Attention Deficit/Hyperactivity Disorder (AD/HD) display a persistent pattern of inattention and/or hyperactivity/impulsivity. AD/HD is a neurologically based disorder that impedes the learning process and interferes with social interactions. Early medical and psycho-educational assessment will help ensure more positive and constructive experiences for the student with AD/HD, as well as for the other students in the class. Usually, a combination of medication, individual and family therapy, support groups, and an Individual Education Plan (IEP) is recommended. If you have a student with AD/HD in your classroom, focus on the student's strengths and teach him or her strategies to complete academic tasks, such as task analysis, and to learn social skills that will enhance interactions with peers and authority figures.

### Characteristics of students with AD/HD

Although students with AD/HD have symptoms of both inattention and hyperactivity-impulsivity, one or the other pattern is predominant. The appropriate subtype should be medically diagnosed. Diagnosis of one of the three subtypes is based on the *Diagnostic and Statistical Manual of Mental Disorders* (fourth edition), commonly known as *DSM — IV*. These subtypes are outlined below.

*AD/HD Combined Type:* Six or more of the symptoms of inattention and six or more of the symptoms of hyperactivity-impulsivity persistently occur in a student's behavior. Most students with AD/HD have the combined type.

*AD/HD Predominantly Inattentive Type:* Six or more of the symptoms of inattention, but fewer than six of the symptoms of hyperactivity-impulsivity persistently occur in a student's behavior.

*AD/HD Predominantly Hyperactive — Impulsive Type:* Six or more of the symptoms of hyperactivity-impulsivity, but fewer than six of the symptoms of inattention persistently occur in a student's behavior.

# What to Look for in Students Suspected of Having AD/HD

When observing a student you suspect of having AD/HD, make systematic observations (see Chapter 1). Note the frequency of behaviors over a period of six months. If a student is suspected of having AD/HD, clusters of behaviors will be observed *often*.

## Inattention

❑ fails to give close attention to details or makes careless mistakes in schoolwork or other related activities. Work is often messy and performed without considered thought.

❑ has difficulty sustaining attention in tasks or play activities

❑ does not seem to listen when spoken to directly

❑ does not follow through on instructions and fails to finish schoolwork, chores, or duties (This is due to inattention and not to a failure to understand instructions.)

❑ has difficulty organizing tasks and activities

❑ avoids, dislikes, or is reluctant to engage in tasks that require sustained mental effort, such as homework or paperwork

❑ loses things necessary for tasks or activities, e.g., toys, school assignments, pencils, books, or tools

❑ is easily distracted by extraneous stimuli that are usually and easily ignored by others, e.g., a car honking, a background conversation

❑ forgetful in daily activities, e.g., missing appointments, forgetting to bring a lunch

## Hyperactivity

❑ fidgets with hands or feet or squirms in seat

❑ leaves seat in situations in which remaining seated is expected

❑ runs about or climbs excessively at inappropriate times (In adolescents or adults this may be limited to subjective feelings of restlessness.)

❑ has difficulty playing or engaging in leisure activities quietly

❑ acts as if "on the go" or as if "driven by a motor"

❑ talks excessively

## Impulsivity

❑ blurts out answers before questions have been completed

❑ has difficulty waiting for his or her turn

❑ interrupts or intrudes on others, for example, butts into conversations or games

Adapted from *Diagnostic and statistical manual of mental disorders* (4th ed.), 1994, Washington, DC: American Psychiatric Association. Used by permission.

Your observations may be an important first step in an assessment process that could lead to the diagnosis and treatment of AD/HD. However, a student must exhibit many of the characteristics over a longer period of time — not just a two-week period. As well, keep in mind that some of these characteristics may be due to other factors, such as the child's developmental stage or high anxiety (such as we saw with Alex in Chapter 2).

## How to Help Students with AD/HD

One of the most important things you can do to help any student with AD/HD is to provide a *structured and predictable* environment.

After she reflected upon her own practices, Alex's teacher used these techniques (see Chapter 3).

*Problem: Fidgety Behavior* — Seat the fidgety student near you when you're teaching so that you may monitor her behaviors. When giving instructions, make eye contact with the student; say, write, and demonstrate what is to be done; and have the student repeat the instructions back to you. Place the student in a desk away from others during seatwork, if necessary, to reduce the amount of sensory stimulation or to decrease the disruption to the other students.

When the students are engaged in activities, observe the fidgety student often for signs of fatigue or loss of interest and stop the activity before it breaks down. As well, ignore minor misbehaviors, such as pencil tapping. Always ask yourself: "Is this bothering me or the entire class?" You will frequently find that during the time you pause to mentally ask this question, the behavior has stopped. You will also discover that more often than not the misbehavior is bothering only you. Unless you ignore minor misbehavior, you will end up nagging the student, and she will likely ignore you. If you must speak to the student about fidgety behavior, do so in a quiet and calm voice.

*Problem: Short Attention Span* — The approach to working with a student with a short attention span is to plan your lessons carefully, monitor the student's behaviors, and give positive feedback. When developing your lessons, plan a variety of activities, such as teacher-directed, small-group, and individual work. Use a multisensory approach, for example, say and write important points and use manipulatives in math and science. Cue the student that it is time to listen and look him in the eye. Involve the student as much as possible in the presentation of the lesson by being your helper or by demonstrating a skill. Keep your presentations short and change activities about every 10 minutes.

Explain seatwork clearly. For example, in math write the assignment on the board and say it to the class. Then do the first question on the board to show the students how to set up their work. You can use the *say*, *write*, and *demonstrate* approach for every subject area. To ensure that the student with a short attention span understands what to do, ask him privately what the assignment is. The student may also benefit by using task analysis (see Chapter 5).

Remember to encourage with praise whenever possible. Say: "I see that most people are listening. This is good because they will hear the instructions. We'll wait for the others to listen too." Praise individual students who are on-task. For example, quietly tell students that you are pleased to see that they are doing what is required and to keep it up. As well, try to schedule interesting or rewarding activities to follow more difficult tasks, for example, a one-minute trip to the water fountain after a reading lesson.

*Problem: Impulsive Approach to Tasks* — Have the student sit near you when you give instructions, make eye contact, and say, "I need you to listen." Make sure that you say, write, and demonstrate all instructions. For example, say, "Write on every second line, place the title in the middle of the top line, and add the date at the left." Then demonstrate this on chart paper or on the board, while repeating it. Next, ask the student to repeat the instructions back to you.

Again, use task analysis, where you break down the tasks into smaller parts, present one part at a time, check the work, offer praise, and assign the next section. Always insist that the student does her best work. When something below standard is submitted and you know the student can do a better job, ask her if this is her best work. Tell her how to improve it while stating that you know she can do a better job.

Sometimes, students complete work in slapdash fashion so that they can be the first to finish or to have time on the computer. Ensure that any student inclined to do this shows you her work before she engages in the other activities. If the work is messy, incomplete, or incorrect, explain how it must be changed and ask her to show it to you when she is finished. The student with AD/HD may require individual assistance to get started on the corrections.

*Problem: Selective Listening* — If the student is not paying attention, ask her to stop what she is doing. Get down to the same level, and when you make eye contact, state the direction clearly, speaking in short sentences. Then ask the student to repeat the instruction back to you. Reinforce the instruction by saying, writing, and demonstrating exactly what you want done. If possible, show the student a sample of a finished product. Monitor the student's progress with the task and give positive reinforcement.

*Problem: Refusal to Complete the Task* — Provide a balky student with individual assistance to help her get started. Sometimes, you may have to compromise on the amount of work assigned. For example, instead of every math question, tell the student to do every second one. However, use this technique sparingly as the child may refuse to work in order to do less.

If you think confidence is an issue, encourage positive self-talk, whereby the child says in his head that he can do the work. Monitor the student's progress with the assignment and encourage him by offering positive feedback.

When you offer choices, you're sharing power with the student and the conflict will de-escalate.

If you feel that the refusal is strictly an issue of power, offer choices to the student. Say: "You can do the work now or for homework. It's your choice. If you choose to do it for homework, you must be quiet so that others will not be disturbed." If the student chooses to do the work later, then it must be noted in his agenda. You *must* check the work the next class. If it is not done, then consequences are administered, for example, loss of marks, a detention, or a phone call home.

*Problem: Wandering in the Classroom* — Allow regular movement breaks so that the student can release energy. Sharpening a pencil one or two times during a designated period (perhaps the time between morning recess and lunch) may serve as a break. If necessary, give the student two pencil passes, one to be given to you every time she gets up to sharpen a pencil. If you use breaks for pencil sharpening or getting a drink, make sure that the student knows the rules during the breaks: remaining in the classroom, being quiet, and keeping her hands to herself.

Another technique is self-monitoring, where the child makes tally marks to record the number of times she is out of her seat. You also keep track and compare your numbers at the end of the period or other agreed-upon amount of time. While self-monitoring may not eliminate the behavior, it usually serves to draw it to the student's attention, which may help to reduce it.

Alex's teacher came to realize that she hadn't consistently followed this rule and may thereby have contributed to Alex's habit of speaking out of turn (see Chapter 3).

*Problem: Calling Out in Class* — When you are questioning your students, insist on the hands-up rule. Cue students by prefacing your questions with the phrase, "Raise your hand if you can tell us . . ." You can also use a visual cue, such as pointing to your arm. Ignore the responses that are spoken out of turn. You *must* call only on those students who raise their hands. When you see the student with AD/HD raise his hand, call on him immediately to reinforce the link between hand raising and answering.

*Problem: Disorganization* — To help a younger student organize her books and materials, place everything in a large plastic tub beneath the desk. Ask older students to color-code their textbooks and binders or to keep morning subjects in one binder and afternoon subjects in another. Another technique is to permit the student to have a set of textbooks at home and one for school, which eliminates forgetting.

To help a younger student organize time, post the weekly schedule in the classroom and follow it. Older students should have multiple copies of their timetable, keeping them in their pencil case, binders, and locker, and at home. When assigning work, tell the students how much time they will have to complete it. When 10 minutes remain in the period, say, "There are 10 minutes left." Also do this when only five and two minutes remain.

Write the homework in the same spot every day and review it orally with the class. Give the students time to copy it into their agendas. You may have to sign the agenda of the student with AD/HD to ensure that the homework is recorded and to show the parents that you have checked it.

Be sure to follow up on assigned homework. Check notebooks often and give marks for neatness and completeness. Some students also find it helpful to have access to a model notebook to check the order of notes and to borrow notes for photocopying. As well, provide class time for students to place handouts where you want them.

## Review Your Own Behavior

You will likely be aware of the behaviors of those students who show signs of AD/HD or of defiance long before you notice the behaviors of those who may be withdrawn. When identifying these students, make careful, systematic observations over four to six months (see Chapter 1). Share your data with the special education teacher or the principal to determine if assessment procedures should be done. Read the student's file to see if there is a history of a particular behavior. As well, describe the behaviors to the parents and inquire as to whether the student shows them at home. Be aware that, if a parent responds that the behaviors are not shown at home, (1) the behaviors may represent a peer or academic problem or (2) the parent is in denial. In either case, you may not have much support at home for your actions. This will limit your success in helping the student demonstrate appropriate behaviors.

Remember to examine your *own* behaviors, too. Ask yourself if you're ever intolerant or impatient. Consider what you can do to make the classroom more *positive, consistent,* and *secure* for all students. Sometimes, you have to make changes in your teaching techniques in order to bring about positive changes in the students' behaviors.

It takes courage to critically assess your methods and make changes that will promote an environment in which behavior problems cannot thrive. That you have read this chapter shows that you are willing to make some changes, if necessary, to help students with behavior problems perform better in your classroom.

# CHAPTER 7

# Visual Impairment

Many of us have impaired vision caused by refractive errors, such as *myopia* (nearsightedness) or *hyperopia* (farsightedness), and these are corrected by prescription lenses. *Visual impairment* refers to serious visual problems that range from an inability to read newsprint with the use of ordinary glasses to total blindness. Problems are also said to occur with *acuity* (sharpness of images) and *field of vision* (range of vision). A person is considered legally blind if he or she has visual acuity of 20/200 or less in the better eye with best correction (such as prescribed glasses or contact lenses). In simple terms, the person sees at 20 feet what people with normal vision see at 200 feet. Problems in field of vision can range from seeing just a pinhole in the middle of the field to seeing only the periphery and not the middle of the image.

Students who cannot benefit from the use of print material are considered to be functionally *blind*. These students must rely on their auditory and tactile senses to learn. They typically read braille, a system of raised characters, and use a cane for mobility. Some students may have an adaptation to a laptop computer that allows them to type braille and to print their work in English for the teacher.

Students who have visual impairment, but who can read print are considered to have *low vision*. Their visual acuity is 20/70 or less in the better eye with best possible correction. These students require accommodations or special equipment to enlarge the print or to adjust the contrast (e.g., magnifying glasses, closed circuit TV, or software). Although most students with low vision will use print, some will also use braille.

In the school-age population, approximately 0.06 percent of students are classified as visually impaired. Of these, about one-quarter are blind. Therefore, over the span of your teaching career, it is likely that you will have a student with visual impairment in your class.

A brailler looks like a small, manual typewriter and produces raised braille characters.

Such a child should already have an Individual Education Plan (IEP) because a student who is blind or has low vision will likely have been identified before entering your classroom. The IEP for a blind student will state that the student is learning braille and will require a brailler or special computer, as well as assistance in the classroom. The IEP for a student with low vision will contain a report from an ophthalmologist and an assessment of the student's functional vision. The medical report provides a diagnosis of the general condition, whereas the assessment on functional vision explains how the student with low vision uses his vision in the classroom. This assessment is important because two people with the same eye condition may use their vision in different ways. A student's vision in the classroom may be determined by motivation, fatigue, and intelligence, as well as a number of environmental circumstances, such as lighting, glare, and contrast. By reading the IEP, you will gain an idea of the student's particular needs.

## Teaching Students Who Are Blind

Students who are blind rely on their auditory and tactile senses to learn; hence, teachers should use a multisensory approach to teaching. These students need to develop a sense of independence and to learn to advocate for themselves, and you can play a role in promoting this (see page 86). Blind students will likely need more time to complete tasks and may need the occasional assistance of a buddy.

The major adjustment for you, as the teacher, will be to work with other adults in the classroom and to prepare lessons well ahead of time. A blind student will require the assistance of a person to braille material for him or her. Therefore, you must be sufficiently organized to give the lesson materials to the consultant to braille for the student before the lesson.

Here are some practical suggestions, some from the Ottawa-Carleton District School Board, on how to teach students who are blind:

- Use as many specific auditory cues as possible. For example, say, "The books are on the top shelf to your right" as opposed to "The books are over there."
- Give specific instructions, such as "Roll the large round ball slowly forward to your partner."
- Repeat instructions and check for understanding by having the child say them back to you. Remember that the child relies more heavily on auditory clues than others.
- As often as possible, teach concepts, such as roughness, using concrete objects. Have the child feel things, such as a rock or Velcro, with his hands. If the child is hesitant, provide hand-over-hand assistance.
- Maintain high behavioral expectations for the student. Do not coddle or allow the use of blindness as an excuse for not doing appropriate tasks.
- At the beginning of the day or the class, outline the agenda to students especially so that the blind child will have an idea of what to expect.
- When calling on other students to give an answer, be sure to say students' names so that the blind student can associate the sound of the people's voices with their names.
- Maintain high academic expectations for the child based on the IEP and what you know he or she can do.
- Provide extra time to complete assignments, if required. Always agree to a specific date or time for the submission of an assignment.
- Pair the student with a buddy who will dictate notes that are written on the board and homework.
- Apply the same rules and consequences to the student who is blind as to the other students.

- If necessary, ask the student to lift his head and face you when speaking. Some children have mannerisms, such as spinning, clapping, or humming. Encourage the child to stop these as they can hinder social acceptance by other students. The student should stand in line, take turns, and keep his desk tidy like every other student.
- Encourage the student to be independent and to advocate for himself.

Beyond adopting the suggestions listed above, communicate regularly with the student's parents. Parents can be an excellent source of information about their child's condition and about effective teaching techniques. It's always a good idea to meet the student and his parents *before* school begins to share information and to establish a viable means of communicating, for example, by e-mail, by the student's agenda, or by telephone.

Plan to meet often with the assistants or consultants who will be working with the child in the classroom. These people teach the child braille and will braille materials for the child. Your job is to be organized and to inform them of lessons ahead of time so that material may be brailled for the student. Older students don't usually require intensive classroom assistance if they have the technology that allows them to scan print material into braille (an Opticom), hear material presented on the computer (a speech synthesizer), or convert braille into English for the teacher (a Navigator).

A final consideration is to ensure a safe and convenient environment. The student needs to be familiar with the physical organization of the classroom. If you change the position of the desks, give him a tour before class. As well, ensure that all aisles are free of clutter and that doors and drawers are closed to avoid tripping or bumping. Assign the student a locker in a convenient location, such as just outside the classroom door. Also, allot a specific space for his brailler or computer and large brailled textbooks.

---

### Promoting Independence and Self-Advocacy

The student who is blind or who has low vision needs to be able to function as independently as possible in your classroom, in the school, and in the community. You can promote independent mobility by providing a safe and predictable physical environment in which the student can use his cane or other device. The student who is blind will likely have received mobility training from a consultant and should be allowed to move independently, even up and down staircases. You can also promote understanding in the student by providing much oral discussion on important ideas and specific directions.

Encourage the student to understand and accept his disability and to identify what teaching techniques work for him. Ask the student if your teaching methods benefit him and if not, invite him to tell you what you might do. Be aware that sometimes, with fatigue or a change of rooms and lighting conditions, what was effective earlier in the day may not work later. Be prepared to change your techniques if necessary. Encourage the student to ask for specific accommodations, such as extra time, on his own. Developing the ability to request accommodations comfortably is a skill that the student will use for the rest of his life.

## Teaching Students with Low Vision

Some ideas on how to teach students who are blind are also applicable to students with low vision. For example, it's valuable to communicate regularly with parents and consultants about your successes and concerns. Specifically, consultants may be able to provide you with strategies for promoting students' residual vision. As with students who are blind, encourage those with low vision to advocate for themselves: they are best able to know what they need.

Most ideas for teaching students with low vision centre on making words larger and clearer. Use large writing on the chalkboard, keeping in mind that for maximum contrast, white and yellow chalk work best on green boards. Keep your boards clean! Enlarge handouts, which should feature well-spaced, dark printing on opaque paper (shiny paper produces glare). Provide photocopies of transparencies because these are particularly hard to read. Choose big books, large-print books, and books on tape to make books more accessible. Encourage the student to use any helpful reading aids, such as magnifying glasses.

Tests may pose particular problems for the student with low vision. When giving tests, read aloud the instructions to the class. Provide extra time for the student with low vision, if required. Also, consider accommodating the student by doing some tests orally. More time and the option to present orally are also appropriate accommodations for assignments.

You will probably need to make some adaptations when it comes to copying material. Have the student copy as much as possible within the given time period, but hand out a copy of the notes to relieve the stress of not completing the task. Another possibility is to give the student a copy of the note in which key words are left out. The student then reads the note and fills in the blanks. Rather than have the student copy extensive notes or diagrams, provide the diagram or map and simply let the child label it. Find alternative tasks to those that require prolonged attention to visual details; otherwise, the student will get very tired.

Discuss needs with the student privately. Each child with low vision has unique requirements that can vary at any time of the day; hence, flexibility on your part and regular communication are necessary. One thing that you can be sure of, though, is that the student will require space to hold special equipment, such as large books, a computer, and reading stands. Let the student experiment with lighting, size and color of pens and pencils, chalk, and print. If you think some tasks may be unsuitable for the student, then discuss your concerns and together develop accommodations or alternate activities. Permitting the student to work with a buddy who can answer questions or provide information about homework or assignments should prove helpful.

Be sure to provide opportunities for social integration. Let the student who has limited vision take on a leadership role, do group work, and more. Doing so will encourage him to see himself as a contributing member of the class, and others will view him in that way too. It's important that *all* the students in your classroom feel that they truly belong.

## Be Attuned to Varying Needs

Knowing that a student has a visual impairment is not enough. You need to be aware of the student's *specific* needs. Remember that teaching accommodations may vary throughout the day so be sure to check with the student. The important thing to remember is that the student benefits from a multisensory method of teaching that emphasizes auditory and tactile channels. He also needs to function as independently in the classroom as possible and to learn self-advocacy skills. Finally, as is true of dealing with all students with exceptionalities, it's important that you work with parents and consultants to learn more about the student's needs and how to work with him.

# CHAPTER 8

# Hearing Impairment

*Hearing loss* is a broad term used to describe a range of hearing impairment. The term *hard-of-hearing* refers to a loss of hearing in the mild to moderate range. A person who is hard-of-hearing generally has sufficient residual hearing that, when wearing a hearing aid, she is able to process oral language. *Deaf* is a term used to refer to hearing losses in the severe and profound range. Many people who are deaf communicate through sign language, a form of manual communication. However, others have had auditory verbal therapy, and when fitted with hearing aids or a cochlear implant, they are able to understand oral language through speech reading and amplification or electromechanical interventions.

## Ways of Improving Hearing

Hearing aids simply amplify sound; they do not restore hearing. Since they amplify *all* sound, including background noise, they do not necessarily make it clearer, just louder. People with mild or moderate hearing loss benefit from the use of hearing aids which are made to individual specifications and are generally worn behind the ear.

Cochlear implants are designed for people with severe to profound hearing loss. An externally worn microphone picks up sound in the environment, amplifies it, and digitizes it into coded signals. These signals are transmitted to the implanted receiver, which stimulates the implanted electrodes in the cochlea. The electrical sound information that is produced is transmitted to the brain for interpretation. When a person has a cochlear implant, that person undergoes *auditory verbal therapy* which involves learning how to speech read and to use his or her hearing to understand spoken language. The person is also taught how to speak.

While in the classroom, students with hearing aids and cochlear implants will likely use an FM system, which consists of a microphone worn by the teacher and a receiver used by the child. Again, this system merely amplifies all sounds in the classroom; it does not make them clearer.

## Ways of Communicating

When hearing loss is detected in a child, parents must select the method of communication. Some parents choose sign language, and children who communicate using sign language will have an interpreter in the classroom. An interpreter is a person who signs the teacher's speech for the child with hearing impairment. Other parents, particularly those who have had their child fitted with hearing aids or cochlear implants, select speech as the method of communication. In order to teach the child to make use of her hearing and to speak, the parents begin auditory verbal therapy. They become speech models and learn how to teach listening and speaking. Finally, some children use a combination of speech and sign language.

## Identifying Hearing Loss

A child with moderate, severe, or profound hearing loss will likely be identified before arriving in your classroom. That student will also have an IEP. However, students with mild hearing loss sometimes go undetected for several years. They are sometimes mistakenly referred for assessment as having behavior problems, learning disabilities, or speech problems. Also, some pre-teens and teens with a hearing impairment choose not to wear their hearing aids. Symptoms of hearing loss that you should be aware of are outlined on the next page.

## How to Work with Students Who Are Speech Readers

Be sure to take advantage of the student's FM system. Ask for it at the beginning of class and wear it throughout. When students are doing group work, arrange for the student's peers to use the system. Ensure that the speech reader's group works in a quiet environment, such as the hallway or library, where there is little background noise. One good idea is to assign the student with hearing impairment the role of recorder to ensure that he or she understands the points made by the group.

A student who is a speech reader must be able to see your lips. A moustache hides the lips.

When you're talking to the whole class, remember to *face* them, especially the speech reading student who should be sitting close enough to you to hear you as well as possible. Saying the name of the student you are calling upon to speak will help the student with hearing impairment know where to look. You'll find it is best to avoid lengthy lectures because the speech reading student may experience difficulty following them. Excessive use of the overhead projector is also undesirable because, with the lights dimmed, the student will be unable to speech read. After presenting a lesson, check with the student privately to see whether the concepts and instructions have been understood.

Help the student with the hearing impairment by using as many visual aids as possible. Write all important points on the chalkboard, and list all homework, assignments, and test dates in the same place on the board every day. When selecting videos, choose those with closed captioning or with a written script. Do your best to use a monitor that accepts closed captioning. And, when assigning work, use the say, write, and demonstrate method: Ensure that the instructions are written and demonstrate exactly what has to be done instead of merely explaining it.

# Symptoms of Hearing Loss

❑ inattentive during large-group discussions or when oral instructions are given

❑ slow to answer or responds inappropriately to simple questions

❑ appears to be a behavior problem in class

❑ turns the head to one side when trying to listen

❑ asks other people to repeat oral instructions or conversations

❑ avoids group discussions and is reluctant to speak (The person can't hear the words and follow the conversation.)

❑ speaks more loudly or softly than the other students

❑ has immature speech and language that is limited in vocabulary and syntax; speech characterized by slurring, sound omissions, or substitutions and a lack of intonation

❑ spells poorly due to problems hearing the language; may be functioning below potential in school

You can also help the student by providing a buddy: the student's peer can take notes and repeat questions and instructions as necessary. However, it is important to encourage the student to take responsibility for her own work. Maintain high academic and behavior expectations for the child: do not permit hearing loss to become an excuse for incomplete work or poor behavior. Encourage the student to do self-advocacy and to accept responsibility for recharging her FM system and for having extra button batteries for the hearing aid.

You will want to ensure that the student with hearing impairment is accepted by the other children in the class. There are several ways to promote this. You can discuss hearing loss with the class so that they gain a better understanding of it. You can also model acceptance by showing patience when repeating instructions and when listening to the child speak. Finally, encourage the student to participate in extracurricular activities to develop social relations and skills, as well as self-esteem.

As you would with all students who have exceptionalities, communicate regularly with the student's parents and work cooperatively with itinerant teachers, teacher assistants, and consultants.

## How to Work with Students Who Have an Interpreter

The key idea to remember is to speak to the class and not the interpreter. Also, don't rely totally on the interpreter. Learn some signs yourself so that you can communicate directly with the child. To aid the student's acceptance in the class, discuss hearing loss with the other students and explain the interpreter's role. You can foster social integration by calling for small-group work and by encouraging the child to take part in extracurricular activities.

## Focus on Communicating Effectively

Watch out for signs of hearing loss. Most students with hearing impairment will have been identified as infants or toddlers, but, as noted earlier, *mild* hearing loss may go undetected for years. When a young child is identified as having a hearing loss, the parents must decide on a method of communication. Parents choosing speech will have their children with mild or moderate hearing loss fitted with hearing aids. Those children with severe or profound hearing loss and who will become speech users may wear hearing aids or have cochlear implants. Other parents will choose sign language as the means of communication for their children. In North America, American Sign Language is most commonly used.

You should be prepared to work with the child, the parents, and other professionals to make accommodations for any student with hearing impairment. In the classroom, ensure that the child can see your lips, that you're wearing the FM system, and that you use as many visual and tactile aids as possible. Once you have begun implementing these teaching techniques, you will find that teaching a student with hearing impairment is not so different from teaching others.

# CHAPTER 9

# Giftedness

Renzulli's model of giftedness from *What Makes Giftedness* (1979)

*Giftedness* has traditionally referred to superior intelligence as measured by a standardized individually administered test. Students scoring two or more standard deviations above the mean and who show superior performance in an academic area are usually identified as being gifted. *Creative* and *talented*, considered as sub-groups, are not usually recognized, as these abilities cannot be easily measured using a test.

The traditional approach described above has given way to one that is based on the work of Renzulli (1979) and Gardner (1983) who rely less on the results of standardized tests and focus on a variety of indicators of giftedness. Renzulli's model consists of three interlocking clusters of traits: above-average ability, creativity, and task commitment. The interaction of the three elements is the key to creative and productive accomplishments. Gardner has identified eight areas of abilities or gifts that a person may have. These intelligences are logical mathematical, linguistic, musical, spatial, bodily kinesthetic, interpersonal, intrapersonal, and naturalistic. If students were identified as having strengths in a particular area, they would be given opportunities to develop their skills in that area.

The approach based on the Renzulli and Gardner models recognizes that a student is not gifted in every subject area. Those models also focus more on the provision of enrichment for many students who may have varying gifts within the regular classroom, as opposed to the creation of special pull-out programs attended by a few students.

Regardless of the approach, some people feel that no extra programming or accommodations need to be made available to gifted children. However, these students do need adaptations in order for them to reach their full potential and to avoid becoming bored and frustrated in school. Such feelings can lead to underachievement, withdrawn or acting-out behaviors, and a general dislike of school.

You may be in a situation where you will be helping to identify students who are gifted. Some children may be very easy to spot as gifted. However, others who are underachieving, do not speak English, have a disability, are economically disadvantaged, or are culturally different may be more difficult to identify. You will need to make careful observations of these students as their gifts may be masked.

## Identifying Gifted Students

Students who demonstrate many of the characteristics identified on the next page *frequently over time* may be academically gifted. Many children will display these characteristics; what separates the gifted from the bright student is the degree or intensity of the characteristics.

## How to Enrich the Learning of Gifted Students

It's desirable to establish a classroom environment in which gifts are valued. You can do this by modeling acceptance of students who have knowledge and abilities in specific areas that are greater than your own. Permit these students to contribute to discussions or to demonstrate skills in physical education or the arts, instead of discouraging their comments, which may be beyond the comprehension or interest of others.

You can provide enrichment activities in your classroom. For example, if you are studying the solar system in science, you could set up a special area in the classroom for extension and enrichment activities, such as doing word searches or encouraging personal research by providing books or Web site addresses on the solar system. These activities permit students to go deeper into a topic or to work on individual projects. Students whose IEPs call for enrichment and those who have a personal interest in a topic should be encouraged to take part in these activities.

You may be tempted to employ gifted students as teacher aides. Don't. This is not enrichment. Similarly, remember to focus on letting gifted students go deeper and broader into a topic. This can be done by compacting or compressing the curriculum to provide time for a student to work on individual projects. For example, if your students are studying triangles in the junior division, have the student do every second question in the seatwork and correct her answers herself. With the time remaining in the period, she can work on an individual project whereby she examines architecture in Ancient Greece in terms of geometric shapes.

If any students are withdrawn from class for enrichment, avoid having them do all of the work that was missed. Instead, select those assignments or parts of those assignments that embody the most important concepts or skills. The key idea in both of the above suggestions is that students who are identified as gifted do not require endless repetition. Suggestions on providing enrichment for gifted students in the regular classroom appear on pages 96–97. Some may also be appropriate for those who possess gifts in specific areas, but who have not been identified as being gifted.

# Characteristics of Gifted Students

❑ exceptional speed of thought, rapid response to new ideas

❑ ability to learn quickly and to process information correctly; little need for detailed explanations

❑ good memory with apparent lack of need to rehearse

❑ large knowledge base on a variety of topics

❑ advanced problem solving and conceptualization, logical thinking; makes good educated guesses

❑ extensive vocabulary

❑ superior reading ability

❑ intellectual curiosity; asks many questions

❑ shows varied or intense interests

❑ has a vivid imagination

❑ searches for a challenge, looks for more complex ways of doing things, enjoys games of thought, plays with ideas and words

❑ flexibility in thinking: sees other ways of viewing problems and generates original ideas and solutions

❑ persistence and goal-directed behaviors, well-developed attention span, ability to work on a task or project for a long time, ability to delay closure

❑ ability to work independently; has a high tolerance for ambiguity

❑ fondness for elaboration, embellishes ideas, concerned with detail

❑ awareness of relationships among diverse ideas, ability to see connections between parts

❑ may be impatient with slower peers

❑ has a keen sense of humor, idealism, a strong sense of justice, high expectations for self, feelings of being different, exceptional emotional depth and intensity, and sensitivity to the feelings of others (These are considered *affective* characteristics.)

## Gifted students at the elementary level

Permit gifted students to work on independent or small-group research projects that are related to the unit being studied. After the students have completed the class assignment, they may work on their research projects. The topics for these projects should be discussed between you and the student.

If you are studying data management with your class, you could establish a learning contract with each gifted student whereby you and the student discuss the product/outcome (e.g., a report on a survey of students in the school), the process for reaching the goal (e.g., developing the questionnaire, collecting the data and analyzing them), and how the project will be evaluated (e.g., teacher and self-evaluation). One excellent resource on this subject is Janice Leroux and Edna McMillan's *Smart Teaching: Talent in the Classroom and Beyond*.

Sometimes, gifted students may become very involved in a given project or writing assignment. Provide extra time for students to complete it. For example, the students in a Grade 1 class may require 30 minutes to write a three-sentence story and draw a picture; a student who is gifted may require 90 minutes spread over two days to write a five-page story with three detailed illustrations. The student may work on it if she is finished her other work early or she may take it home.

If possible, integrate several disciplines into one unit. For example, integrate an exploration of pulleys and levers, novel study, and medieval history into a unit. Doing this helps the students understand how subject areas may be linked to solve problems or to provide a deeper and broader understanding of a topic. Consider using overarching themes, such as adaptation, community, cooperation, exploration, conflict, heroism, and survival, in order to provide a framework for study and to help the students to understand how many things may be viewed from a different and possibly unusual perspective. For example, with an elementary class you may adopt the themes of survival and adaptation as you study animals in science, pioneers in history, and *Roughing It in the Bush* in language arts.

Instead of a steady diet of questions that ask students merely to recall facts, incorporate higher order thinking skills into your questioning, as well as into the assignments. Ask questions that require students to analyze, synthesize, and evaluate information. (See Bloom's taxonomy for more information.) For example, ask them to describe how two characters in a novel are similar and different (analysis). Or, require students to produce a graphic that embodies the concepts learned in a unit in health (synthesis). You might also have them assess and explain whether certain industrial or agricultural practices are ecologically sound (evaluation). As well, ask students open-ended questions that permit them to speculate on things, such as the ending to a story, or ask "what would happen if."

Encourage gifted students to take on extra responsibilities. For example, one might serve as an editor of a class newspaper or group project. As a teacher, you might also suggest that a student join a club or try out for a school team, the band, or the school musical, if that's where a student's strengths seem to lie.

Maintain high standards of academic work and of behavior. As with all your class, these students should follow the rules and be held accountable for their actions. Beyond the classroom, they could work with a mentor in their field of interest. For example, a student with an interest in creative writing may be given the opportunity to correspond through e-mail with a prominent author or poet.

Briefly, Bloom (1956) identifies six cognitive levels from less complex to more complex: (1) knowledge, (2) comprehension, (3) application, (4) analysis, (5) synthesis, and (6) evaluation. The first two levels are considered to be lower levels of thinking because they involve memorization of information; the remaining levels are higher levels of thinking because the student must demonstrate an understanding of material.

Erik's teachers recognized his strengths in math, computers, and music. They encouraged him to explore these areas further than the regular curriculum by joining the Engineering Club and the Grade 7 Band.

### Gifted students at the secondary level

In the classroom, ask gifted students higher order questions that require more than factual recall. In your questioning and on assignments, ask students to analyze material, synthesize ideas, and evaluate positions. As well, ask open-ended questions that require the students to speculate or predict based on known data. You can also provide opportunities for gifted students to independently investigate topics related to a unit of study. For example, in a unit on light you may permit a student to research the use of lasers in cosmetic surgery or photonics. An extra project could be substituted for another assignment or it could be completed for bonus marks.

Encourage such students to develop leadership skills through courses and workshops and to take an active part in extracurricular activities at school and in the community. Some gifted students will embrace the opportunity to become involved and thrive in balancing a broad range of school and community activities with school work. Other gifted students may want to participate only in specific clubs or activities. Still others may choose not to participate at all. As a teacher, you can highlight specific activities or appeal to a need to socialize, but you cannot make your students join.

Special courses can also provide enrichment opportunities. Encourage gifted students to take not only high school courses at the most advanced level, but to look at non-credit courses that may be offered in the community and credit courses offered at a university. As with clubs, some students will want to take these kinds of courses and others will not.

Gifted students might benefit from taking part in a mentoring program. Before you begin arranging something, talk with a student to determine interest level. Perhaps the student could communicate in person or by e-mail with a prominent person in a field of interest. For example, if you had a student who found social history absorbing and, in particular, the activities of the Women's Christian Temperance Union, you could introduce this student to a historian who shares similar research interests and who would enjoy mentoring the student.

Cooperative education placements can also especially benefit gifted students. They provide opportunities for students to explore career areas to determine suitability and specific areas of interest. For example, a student with an interest in becoming a veterinarian might find it helpful to be placed in an animal shelter. If the student is willing, speak to the guidance office about linking the student with a mentor or finding a placement in a business, office, or lab.

## Encourage Your Students

Gifted students need opportunities for enrichment. Some teachers are reluctant to adapt their teaching style or curriculum because they think it is too much work. The suggestions in this chapter about providing individual projects and opportunities to join clubs or other activities are *easy* to implement. You may find that students who have not been identified as gifted may become interested in participating in the enrichment activities as well. Encourage *all* of your students to develop higher order thinking skills, pursue their interests, and wonder about the possibilities.

# CHAPTER 10

# Developmental Disability

*Developmental disability*, *intellectual disability*, and *mental retardation* are terms used to describe below-average intellectual functioning which is manifested in immature reactions to environmental stimuli and delayed social and academic performance. The definition adopted by the American Association on Mental Retardation (AAMR) is as follows:

> Substantial limitations in personal functioning, characterized by significant subaverage intellectual functioning, existing concurrently with related limitations in two or more of the following adaptive skills: communication, self-care, home living, social skills, community use, self-direction, health and safety, functional academics, leisure, and work. Mental retardation is manifested before age 18 (AAMR, 1993).

Essentially, a person with developmental disability has scored less than 70 on an IQ test and shows significant weaknesses in adaptative behavior. Adaptative behavior refers to how a person responds to the environmental demands, which are affected by age and culture.

Developmental disability is classified into four categories: mild, moderate, severe, and profound. Children with mild and moderate developmental disability are usually placed in regular classrooms with little support. Those with severe and profound developmental disability are placed in special education classrooms and are integrated into regular classrooms to improve social behaviors. These students will be accompanied by a teacher aide, and you will not likely be required to provide educational programs for them. Hence, the focus of this section will be on characteristics and strategies related to *mild* developmental disability.

## Characteristics of Students with Mild Developmental Disability

Most children diagnosed with mild developmental disability will be educated in regular classrooms, with or without the support of a teacher aide or other professional personnel. These students learn at about one-half to three-quarters of the rate of their normally developing peers, and over time, some of these students may be capable of doing work in academic subjects up to the higher elementary grades. General achievement ranges from the second to the fifth grade. Nevertheless, many of these students can be taught functional English and math, and they may learn job-related skills through direct training and supervised cooperative education placements. The checklist on page 100 lists characteristics that may be displayed by students with mild developmental disability in the classroom.

---

### Focus on Down Syndrome

Down syndrome is a genetic defect causing limitations in physical and intellectual development. It is caused by an aberration in chromosome 21: in most cases, there is an extra copy of this chromosome instead of the usual pair (one each from the mother and father). The condition is usually recognized at birth, on the basis of characteristic features or through chromosome testing. Children with Down syndrome typically have some degree of developmental disability — mild, moderate, or severe. Common observable features include upward sloping eyes, a protruding tongue due to a small mouth cavity, a head that is flattened at the back, a short flat nose, short fingers — particularly the fifth — a wide space between the first and second toes, low muscle tone, and a short stocky build. Children with Down syndrome also have higher rates of congenital heart defects and leukemia than the general population.

---

## How to Help Students with Mild Developmental Disability

A transition plan identifies academic and vocational goals for the student and outlines the steps and agencies involved in meeting them.

As with all students who have recognized exceptionalities, do the essential research and work cooperatively with others. Read the IEP and talk to the student's teacher aide, if one has been assigned. Work with other professionals, such as the occupational therapist, resource teacher, reading specialist, speech-language pathologist, and behavior specialist. Meet with the parents or caregivers to discuss the teaching approaches and behavior modification programs that have proved to be effective. Also, discuss the goals the parents have for their child. These become very important during adolescence because transition plans have to be developed and implemented. The transition plan is usually developed by the special education or guidance departments.

One of the most important things you can do in the classroom is to provide a structured, predictable environment. Doing this helps to reduce student anxiety about not knowing what to expect. You can post the weekly schedule in a place that is visible to all the students and *follow it*. At the beginning of the day, point to the day of the week on the schedule and read the subjects that will be taught. Highlight any schedule changes, such as an assembly being held in lieu of social studies. For each lesson, tell the students what will be covered that period.

Transitions from one activity to another are sometimes difficult for students with developmental disability. It is not unusual for them to want to perseverate, or continue on the task past the desired time. One way you can ease transitions is to give a 10-minute warning that you will be finishing one subject and moving on to another. Then give further warnings at the five- and two-minute marks. To reinforce this with the student with developmental disability, go to

# How to Identify Students with Mild Developmental Disability

❑ has a poor memory, e.g., can perform a task one day, but not the next; has difficulty remembering a series of instructions or the sequence of numbers

❑ has immature language patterns and uses simple vocabulary

❑ speech may be delayed and slurred

❑ may have difficulty understanding body language, such as facial expression and tone of voice

❑ has difficulty with abstract concepts, is clearly oriented in the present and not in the past or future

❑ has difficulty generalizing and transferring information to day-to-day activities, e.g., may be able to add, but can't total purchases in a store

❑ displays learned helplessness, reluctant to try new things, and may try to manipulate others to do the task for him or her

❑ requires extrinsic motivation to do things

❑ may be disorganized and has difficulties keeping track of personal belongings

❑ is slow to complete academic work which may be due to slow processing of information and/or short attention span

❑ may have low self-esteem and may make negative statements about self

❑ has difficulty making a transition from one activity to another, for example, moving from recess or physical education back to the classroom

❑ may exhibit specific anxieties, such as going to the washroom, or specific compulsive behaviors

❑ may be aggressive due to lack of success, fear of failure, low self-esteem, resistance to transitions from one activity to another, or excessive stimulation such as is found in a school cafeteria

his desk and quietly ask the student how many minutes are left and what will be done after this activity.

When teaching a lesson, gain the student's attention by directly asking him to look at you. Say quietly, "I need you to look here." Explain why the student needs to know the information or skill you will be teaching and relate it to his own life. In physical education you can say, "When you are playing basketball and you can't make the shot because the defenders are around you, pass the ball. Today, we're going to learn how to do one type of pass." Involve the student as much as possible through hands-on activities and questions. Phrase questions simply and allow sufficient "wait time" for the question to be processed and the answer to be formulated. Encourage the child to use his language by asking open-ended questions that don't require a mere "yes" or "no."

When giving instructions, speak in short, simple sentences and privately ask the student to repeat the instructions. Demonstrate exactly what you want to be done. You may also have to give instructions for this student one at a time and couple each one with positive feedback and, if necessary, a short break. Do the same for tasks. (See the information on task analysis in Chapter 5.) For example, after completing a certain amount of work, praise the student, and permit him to get a drink of water.

When the student is working on assignments, provide him with a buddy. This student's role is to assist with non-instructional tasks, such as applying glue to a craft. You should give as much individual assistance to the student as possible to ensure that he is on-task and understands the work, too.

## Planning lessons for a student with mild developmental disability

A student with developmental disability learns at a slower pace than his peers, and you have to adapt the curriculum to reflect the student's academic and cognitive levels. For example, children in a Grade 1 class may be working with numbers from 10 to 20; however, the student with developmental disability may spend the entire year on numbers from 0 to 10.

Students with developmental disabilities benefit from the use of a multi-sensory approach to teaching. You can teach by discussing important ideas, showing pictures and writing key words, and providing objects that can be touched. For example, if the topic is money and you are teaching about pennies and nickels, tell the students about each of the coins, show pictures and corresponding values, and have them manipulate real coins.

You may also need to shorten assignments by reducing the number of questions to be answered or the amount to be written. If the student has difficulty with fine-motor control, pre-cut materials for crafts or partially assemble the item to avoid frustration with scissors or glue.

As noted in earlier chapters, if copying notes is a problem, give the child a photocopy of the note or a fill-in-the blank version whereby he writes the key words in the spaces. You may also need to provide extra time for the student to complete assignments.

Plan to reinforce learning through repetition. You will need to review skills and information often, as things learned one day may be forgotten the next. One way to do this is by purchasing or preparing games that review such things as the alphabet, the names of the days of the week and the months, basic sight words, and number facts. Software that drills these concepts may also be purchased. Sometimes pairing the student with a patient buddy can turn the review into a game.

Evaluate the student's assignments in light of the goals for the student and the grade level at which he is working. For example, in a Grade 5 class when students are writing a two- to three-page story, the student with developmental disability, who is working at the Grade 2 level, may be required to write three sentences and draw a picture. Regardless of the student's academic level, always maintain high standards for him.

## Managing the behavior of a student with mild developmental disability

Expect the same standard of behavior for the student with developmental disability as you would for the others. All students must be accountable for their behavior and know that you will apply consequences for misbehavior. For example, if the student hits another child during recess, talk to the student about what happened and how the situation should have been handled. Request that the student apologize and direct him to wait alone a few minutes by the school. Signal to him when he may play again.

You will have to review the class rules frequently as they may be forgotten. Praise the student when he follows the rules to reinforce the correct behavior. You should also watch for signs of anxiety and frustration when completing a task. Monitor the student frequently by watching him and going to his desk. If the student appears anxious, suggest a two-minute break or another way to do the task. You might also provide some individual assistance to help him over a difficult section of the work.

To develop appropriate behaviors, adopt the use of a behavior modification plan. If your goal is to have the student complete his work, explain that you will reward finished work with time to read a book or use the computer or with a check mark that may be redeemed for a prize. You can also reduce inappropriate behavior by substituting socially acceptable ones. For example, to reduce unwanted hugging, substitute high fives.

Role playing may also be used to teach appropriate behaviors. If a child is taking the lunch boxes of other students and hiding them, ask him and another student to role-play a situation in which the child with developmental disability is first, the perpetrator, and second, the victim. After each scenario, discuss how the child felt. Then talk about the acceptable behavior, have the child demonstrate it, and praise it. Discuss how it felt to do the right thing and monitor the student during the next lunch break. Encourage the correct behavior and praise him for it.

## Developing self-confidence and social acceptance

Feeling good about ourselves helps motivate us to keep trying. A student with developmental disability needs to develop self-confidence for the same reason. You can help the student by ensuring that there are tasks at which he can succeed, by providing individual assistance, and by insisting that he perform personal tasks, such as putting on his coat by himself, independently.

Keep positive feelings going by discouraging negative self-talk. Many students who have developmental disability claim to be "no good at anything." You need to remind them of their strengths, which may range from being careful to water classroom plants to knowing their number facts. Do not permit any student to engage in negative self-talk.

You can help the student gain social acceptance in a variety of quiet ways. Model accepting behaviors yourself and monitor anxiety levels to avoid a blow-up or tantrum, which can be very embarrassing. A tantrum could also make the other students afraid of the child with developmental disability. Try to monitor classroom activities as closely as possible to ensure that the student is behaving appropriately and that others are not teasing him. If necessary, speak to the class about developmental disability and how their classmate should be treated.

Another method of developing social acceptance is through group work. You should choose a task, such as managing materials, at which the student can succeed. Select group members who are tolerant and patient. Successful group experiences help the student to be seen in a positive light, which may lead to friendships.

## Model Patience and Respect

You may feel awkward about working with a student with developmental disability. But there is no need to feel this way. Read the IEP and talk to others about what approaches are effective. Make note of the student's academic performance and social skills. Sometimes, a student's test scores are lower than actual day-to-day performance. Use the teaching techniques and suggestions for curriculum adaptation to ensure that the student experiences success in your classroom. Have high expectations for the student, but remember that he will learn more slowly than others and will require much more repetition. Knowing this, be patient with the student and model respectful behavior towards him. You will soon find that the other students in the class will do the same.

# CHAPTER 11

# Low-Incidence Disabilities

In this chapter, you will learn about several disabilities that do not occur frequently in the population, but can have a major impact on a student's functioning. These are called *low-incidence disabilities*, and students with these disabilities are frequently educated in the regular classroom. Therefore, it is likely that you will teach at least one student within this broad category of exceptionality in your career. Autism, Asperger's disorder, Tourette syndrome, fetal alcohol syndrome, and physical disabilities are discussed below.

Most of these students will have been identified before entering your classroom and will have an Individual Education Plan (IEP). When working with a student who has a low-incidence disability, it is important to read the child's file to learn about specific strengths and needs. As well, work closely with the student's parents or caregivers. They can provide support for you and information on their child's condition and what teaching techniques are effective. You will also likely need to work with a paraprofessional and other professionals in meeting the requirements of the IEP. One of the most important things you can do for many students is to talk to them privately and ask which techniques are effective.

## Working with Paraprofessionals

Paraprofessionals (also known as educational assistants, teacher aides, and classroom assistants) are often cited as the most important facilitator of integration of children with severe disabilities. In many cases, the paraprofessional implements the academic and behavioral programs for students with severe disabilities.

You and the paraprofessional complement each other. Your role as the classroom teacher is to understand the strengths and needs of the student, know how to adapt instruction and curriculum for the child, develop behavioral management programs, track the progress of the student, evaluate the progress of the student, and report to parents. You are also responsible for disciplining the child, if necessary. The role of the paraprofessional is to *implement* the instructional and curricular adaptations, as well as the behavioral management plan. However, it is recognized as good practice to involve the paraprofessional in planning the accommodations.

The need to work closely with the paraprofessional makes it imperative for you to develop a good working relationship with that person. Begin by communicating regularly and at mutually agreeable times with the paraprofessional, sharing observations, information, concerns, and ideas about working with the student. In some cases, the paraprofessional has worked with a particular student for several years and can contribute valuable information and expertise. Respect the skills and knowledge that the paraprofessional brings to the job.

## Autism

Autism is considered to be a *Pervasive Developmental Disorder* (PDD), meaning that a broad range of domains are affected. With autism, the main affected areas are social interaction as well as verbal and nonverbal communication. When an autistic child reaches school age, educational peformance is also adversely affected. Autism usually presents itself before the age of three, but diagnosis is sometimes slow since no diagnostic test exists. The diagnostic process relies on observation only, and if misdiagnosis occurs (the condition may be mistaken for hearing impairment), the opportunity for critical early intervention is lost.

Autism is a lifelong condition that ranges in degree from severe to mild. A child with severe autism may have no receptive or expressive language; an individual with more sophisticated communication abilities may have a milder form of autism. Autism is caused by genetic factors that predispose the child to developing this condition in which there is damage to the central nervous system and the brain's circuits. It is also associated with X-linked chromosomal abnormalities, in particular, the subtype fragile X.

The main difficulty for a child with autism seems to lie with processing information. Heightened sensitivity to sensory stimuli, inability to process multiple messages simultaneously, and changes to routine may trigger abnormal behavior ranging from withdrawal, which may include rocking, to having tantrums, which include throwing objects, spitting, and headbanging. The child experiences confusion, either retreating into a familiar pattern to gain control over the situation or maybe throwing a tantrum to express frustration and anger. As well, children with autism experience difficulties in communication and in establishing social relationships. Focusing on increasing communication skills and establishing a structured, organized environment helps the child to make progress in the classroom setting.

## How to Help Students with Autism

Read the student's file and pay particular attention to the IEP in order to determine specific academic and social strengths and needs. The student may not be working at grade level and may require modifications to the curriculum. However, when considering teaching strategies for a child with autism, four elements are critical: structure, organization, routine, and consistency. Children with autism become extremely agitated when things are out of order and routine is not followed. Hence structure and consistency are very important to make the environment predictable and to develop a sense of control within the child. These become the stable foundation from which the student can learn.

### Establishing routines

Post the class schedule in a spot in the classroom so that all of the students can see it. If required, use pictures to show the schedule or pictures and words. At the beginning of each day, review what subjects will be covered especially so that the student with autism will know what to expect. Avoid deviating from the schedule as much as possible. However, sometimes changes are necessary. Inform the students about the time of any assembly and mention what will be missed. Be prepared to answer questions about the event throughout the day. If at all possible, find out when the fire drills will be scheduled and warn your students about them on the appropriate days. Tell them that you can't predict at what time the drill will occur, but that there will be one. Remind them about how to behave during a drill.

Some students with autism perseverate, or continue an action beyond a reasonable time. These actions could be rocking back and forth, stroking a lock of hair, sucking a thumb, or manipulating an object. There may be times when, due to the nature of the child or task or his mood, your student with autism will not want to stop an academic activity and move on to the next one. You will need to give a warning about when the activity will change. For example, when 10 minutes remain in the period, tell the students that you will be finishing language and moving to math in 10 minutes. Repeat the warnings at the five- and two-minute marks.

### Curriculum modification and teaching strategies

When planning lessons, know the student's strengths and needs. The child may be functioning at grade level in some areas and at a different level in others. Plan activities at which you know the student can succeed. You may have to modify some in order to ensure success. For example, if you are planning a craft activity, you may want to pre-cut materials and have the teacher aide provide individual assistance in the assembly of the craft. If possible, consider structuring the activities so that a non-preferred activity is followed by a preferred one.

Plan to teach your lessons using a multisensory approach. Say the important points, write key ideas on the board or on chart paper, and use concrete objects to teach concepts. When presenting the material, use short, simple sentences and involve the child as much as possible by asking questions and inviting him to touch the objects. Plan on repeating key ideas and develop drill activities or purchase software that will reinforce concepts and facts.

During the seatwork part of the lesson, ensure that the child receives individual attention. Depending on the severity of the autism, you or a teacher aide may provide this one-to-one attention. If necessary, use verbal or physical prompts when guiding the child's performance of a task. For example, place your hands on the child's to trace or say aloud the instructions, such as, "cut, back, cut, back" when using scissors. Fade out or withdraw the prompts to encourage independent performance. Consider, too, the value of task analysis whereby you break the work into smaller tasks and give positive feedback after each is completed. As well, provide a short break if you notice that the student is becoming agitated or frustrated with the work.

### Encouraging communication

Use a variety of communication methods with the student: oral, gestural, pictorial, and written. These methods may be used in combination. For example, when gaining the student's attention, move close to the child, say his name, then give simple instructions orally and combine them with gestures. When asking questions, allow for wait time as the child may be slow in responding. Comment frequently on the environment and what is happening around you to provide information and encourage social interaction. Elaborate on the child's utterances. For example, if the student says, "Hat," say, "Yes, you have a new baseball cap." Encourage the child to communicate his feelings as this may alleviate any anger and frustration. Discuss the vocabulary for feelings to give the words for happy, sad, disappointed, frustrated, and angry. Some children may find that using pictures and words helps them to communicate their feelings.

### Behavior

Establish reasonable expectations that the child can meet. State the expected behaviors in positive terms and be prepared to enforce the rules several times before the child realizes that you are committed to them. Provide positive feedback for appropriate behaviors, perhaps by spoken comments, the use of pictures, such as a happy face, or gestures, such as a raised thumb, or by both verbal and visual means.

If the student misbehaves, be sure to implement logical consequences. For example, if he spills the paint, then provide a sponge for him to clean it up. Show him how to do it and ensure he cleans up the mess. If necessary, set up a behavior modification plan for the child. Find out what motivates the child and use those "carrots" to reinforce appropriate behavior. Plan a menu of reinforcers from which the child may choose.

When it comes to students with autism becoming agitated and having a tantrum or blow-up, take a preventative approach. Regularly observe the child for signs of anxiety and divert his attention or provide a break to relieve the stress. You may also consider providing individual assistance or restructuring a task if it proves to be too difficult at that time. As well, monitor the child's interactions with other students to ensure that they say nothing that will create extreme agitation.

## Asperger's Disorder

Asperger's disorder is a diagnosis applied when a child displays severe social behavior deficits and a restricted pattern on interests and activities. Like autism, Asperger's disorder is a lifelong developmental condition which is characterized by a severe and sustained impairment in social interaction and the development of restricted, repetitive patterns of behavior, interests and activities. However, unlike autism, children with Asperger's disorder do not have significant delays in language, general cognitive development or age-appropriate self-help skills, and adaptive behavior (other than social interaction).

A child with Asperger's disorder will display a lack of sensitivity to others, as well as weakness in social understanding. The child will lack empathy and speak by proclaiming or declaring rather than by engaging in two-way conversation. He or she may talk in a monotonous tone of voice, be overly precise, and ramble on endlessly. The child's interests tend to be idiosyncratic or

A menu of reinforcers could include 15 minutes on a computer, an opportunity to stay in during one recess with a friend or to play with a particular ball, or a 15-minute pass to the library. Consider developing the menu with the child to ensure that the reinforcers are appropriate; be prepared to change them if they no longer motivate the student.

When you state the rules by beginning with "Don't," you are telling the student what not to do. He is left with having to guess at what behavior you want, and it may take several attempts to figure out exactly what you expect. Try stating exactly what behavior is appropriate in the classroom and before a special event.

circumscribed, a fascination with maps being one example. He or she may repeat words or phrases and become attached to certain repetitive activities.

On the other hand, a student with Asperger's disorder will have an IQ in the normal or high range and possess an excellent long-term and rote memory. He or she may be able to read or memorize passages or items, but may display little comprehension.

## How to Help Students with Asperger's Disorder

Read the student's file and pay particular attention to the IEP in order to determine specific academic and social strengths as well as needs. Structure is important for children with Asperger's disorder. Therefore, ensure that the students know the class schedule and routines and that you consistently follow them.

When teaching, use a multisensory method in which you present concepts using the oral, visual, and tactile channels (see Chapter 5). Involve the child as much as possible during the presentation of the lessons through questioning or being a helper. When giving instructions, state specifically what you want done and demonstrate how it is to be done. If necessary, use task analysis to break down the work into smaller tasks. Give positive feedback as each segment is completed.

Outline the expected behaviors to the student, and reinforce correct behaviors with positive feedback. Use logical consequences for inappropriate behaviors. For example, if the child chooses not to work on the assignment in class, then it will be for homework. Watch for signs of anxiety and when you see them, redirect the student to another task, provide individual assistance, suggest that the student take a water break, or modify the task.

Some students with Asperger's disorder have difficulty socializing with peers. They may speak in a pedantic, declarative way that offers little opportunity for two-way conversation. During large-group discussions, discourage overly long comments by suggesting that you and the student discuss the topic at another time. You might also consider seating the student next to a peer who is easygoing and tolerant and who has well-developed social skills. Structure academic tasks so that discussion about the topic will occur and permit some off-task conversation as well. Use cooperative learning techniques whereby in group work students have specified tasks. Ensure that the student with Asperger's disorder is assigned a variety of tasks beginning with the ones you know can be done successfully.

You may also want to do some role playing with the student to teach social skills. You can have the student play the perpetrator and then the victim in a scenario and discuss the feelings of the people in both roles. During the next few days, quietly remind the child of the appropriate behavior, monitor the behavior, and provide positive feedback for appropriate behaviors and logical consequences for inappropriate behavior.

## Tourette Syndrome

Tourette syndrome is a neurological disorder in which there are deficiencies in the person's inhibitory circuits which would normally suppress certain inappropriate behaviors (e.g., obsessive-compulsive). It's important to note that these deficiencies are due to underdevelopment of the circuits and not to poor parenting. Some people are genetically vulnerable to Tourette syndrome, while others might develop it due to some cause such as a lack of oxygen.

This syndrome is characterized by tics — involuntary muscular movements, uncontrollable vocal sounds, and/or inappropriate words. The symptoms usually appear between the ages of two and 21; however, diagnosis usually occurs after age seven. They wax and wane according to stages in development and the particular situation and are the greatest during mid-adolescence and the twenties. The symptoms may also be more prominent in situations in which the child is nervous or is annoyed by the behavior of others (e.g., domineering behaviors of others). However, by the time the person is in his or her mid-twenties, the circuits usually catch up in development and the tics become inhibited. The person may also have learned coping strategies. It should be noted that as yet there is no cure, although medication will often control the symptoms.

The severity of the disorder and the concomitant disabilities will determine to a large extent how the child does in school. Besides verbal or physical tics, a student with Tourette syndrome may have AD/HD, learning disabilities, and obsessive-compulsive behaviors. (See Chapters 5 and 6 for suggestions about specific needs associated with these conditions.) The student with Tourette syndrome requires a compassionate environment with support from the teacher and peers to help cope with the academic, social, and emotional problems that may arise. As well, these students need to accept themselves, learn coping strategies, and develop self-esteem.

## How to Help Students with Tourette Syndrome

One of the most important things you can do is to acknowledge that the student has to tic and be accepting of the student and tolerant of the tics and possible rituals. You may want to discuss Tourette syndrome with the others in the class, and tell them to ignore the tics. Always model respectful behavior towards the student and monitor others' behaviors towards the child to ensure that no teasing occurs. Be sure, too, to talk with the student regularly to see how your practices are working.

In the classroom, provide breaks for the student to get away and tic after a certain amount of time. For example, permit the student to leave to go to the washroom or to get a drink so that he can tic in relative privacy. You may also want to seat the student at the back of the room where he can tic without disturbing others. Ask older students where they would like to sit to provide them with some control over the situation. You may also consider establishing a private signal with the student that will tell you when he needs to get away to tic. Encourage the student to disguise a tic so that it looks like an everyday movement, such as brushing the side of the nose.

Plan group work using cooperative learning techniques. When tasks are assigned, ensure that the student with Tourette syndrome is assigned something he can do. It's desirable that the student's peers view him as competent.

Do your best to be aware of any medication that the student may be taking. Find out about possible side effects, for example, sleepiness, fatigue, restlessness, depression, and any unusual difficulty in learning. Try to take these into account.

Some older students with Tourette syndrome may become discouraged about their disability. They may lack self-esteem and confidence. You might suggest that the guidance or special education department of your school help the student find a mentor who also has Tourette syndrome and who has achieved a measure of success. The student and the mentor could communicate through e-mail, by telephone, or in person.

## Fetal Alcohol Syndrome/Effects

Fetal alcohol syndrome/effects (FAS/E) is a condition found in some children of mothers who consumed large amounts of alcohol during pregnancy. Children with FAS are known to have developmental disability, specific physical characteristics, and neurological abnormalities. It is thought that the alcohol kills brain cells, which results in a smaller-sized brain and specific facial features. These facial features include small eyes, a small head circumference (microcephaly), and a short nose with a flat bridge. A continuum of developmental defects exists, from full-blown FAS to FAE, caused by maternal drinking during pregnancy, but not showing all of the symptoms of FAS.

Children with FAS/E are often identified by their teachers due to their learning and behavior needs. While each child with FAS/E is unique with special strengths and needs, a typical profile of a child with FAS/E can be described using the acronym LLAMA. A child with FAS/E will likely show some characteristics in all of the categories outlined on the next page.

When suggesting to the parents that they consult with their family physician, be sensitive to and respectful of the family's situation. The child may be living with a birth, adoptive, or foster family.

## How to Help Students with FAS/E

Establishing structure and routines in your classroom is important. Post the class schedule and follow it. When assemblies, photo sessions, and the like are scheduled, inform the students at the beginning of the day and explain how the event will affect the regular schedule. Have routines for lining up, passing out materials, submitting work and doing other activities that occur several times a day. Be sure to follow these routines yourself.

As you plan lessons, consider using a multisensory method in which you incorporate oral, visual, and tactile learning channels. Plan activities in which the student will be successful, and if necessary, reduce academic expectations. During instruction, seat the student close to you so that you may keep him involved and focused. Explain why the child needs to know the information or skill that is being taught and relate it to his life as much as possible. Make very specific instructions for the seatwork, using short, simple sentences, and demonstrate exactly what is to be done.

During the activity, go to the student's desk, ask him to repeat the directions, and watch him begin his work. Gently correct if necessary and offer positive feedback. You might break the work into smaller tasks and offer positive feedback as each segment is completed. Watch for signs of anxiety, ready to provide individual assistance, offer a break to get a drink, or redirect the activity. For further suggestions, see Chapter 5 on learning disabilities, Chapter 6 on behavioral disorders, and Chapter 10 on developmental disability.

# Recognizing a Child with FAS/E

**Learning Disabilities**
- ❑ reading disabilities: early reading difficulty, later problems with comprehension
- ❑ written language disabilities: spelling, creative writing
- ❑ mathematics disabilities: difficulty learning math facts, telling time, solving problems
- ❑ difficulty with abstract concepts
- ❑ difficulty generalizing information from one situation to another

**Language Delay/Disorders**
- ❑ immature speech/language
- ❑ overly "chatty" but with no substance
- ❑ difficulty following oral instructions
- ❑ slow to process language
- ❑ overly concrete or literal in understanding of language; difficulty with abstract concepts; misinterprets language messages

**Attention Deficit/Hyperactivity**
- ❑ restless and fidgeting
- ❑ short attention span and easily distracted in the middle of a task
- ❑ easily overstimulated and overwhelmed, leading to outbursts
- ❑ impulsive — acts without thinking of possible consequences; doesn't anticipate danger

**Memory**
- ❑ good long-term memory for past events, but can't remember what happened this morning
- ❑ concepts learned one day are forgotten by the next
- ❑ established daily routines may be forgotten
- ❑ difficulty with sequential thinking
- ❑ weak short-term memory
- ❑ difficulty with retrieval of information unless prompted

**Adaptive Behavioral Concerns**
- ❑ difficulty understanding cause/effect — thinking seems "illogical"
- ❑ requires more repetitions than normal to learn from consequences
- ❑ difficulty perceiving social "cues," thereby alienating peers
- ❑ social skills are immature
- ❑ easily manipulated and led by others
- ❑ blames others; egocentric
- ❑ doesn't seem to accept that rules apply to him or her
- ❑ mood swings
- ❑ may over- or under-react to situations
- ❑ overly tactile beyond the age where acceptable; inappropriate touching a possible problem
- ❑ difficulty adapting to changes, perseverative or "stubborn"
- ❑ difficulty making choices
- ❑ overly friendly and affectionate — easily approached by strangers

Adapted from *Awareness of Chronic Health Conditions*. © 2000 Province of British Columbia. All rights reserved. Reprinted with permission of the Province of British Columbia

# Physical Disabilities

Physical disabilities range from mild to severe and may be caused by genetic abnormalities or prenatal, perinatal, or postnatal factors. Cerebral palsy, spina bifida, and muscular dystrophy will be discussed in this section. None of these conditions is contagious, and only muscular dystrophy is degenerative. At this time no long-term cure for any of these conditions exists.

### Cerebral palsy

Cerebral palsy is caused by damage to the brain before, during, or just after birth and results in motor disorders (fine and large muscle control), sensory disorders (sight and hearing), and sometimes cognitive impairment. The continuum of defects ranges from no obvious physical difficulties or a minor speech impairment to severe motor problems resulting in no mobility and total lack of speech. Despite the brain damage, most children with cerebral palsy have normal intellectual functioning and are able to learn in a regular classroom. As well, most care for themselves and walk unaided.

### Spina bifida

Spina bifida, a congenital defect occurring during the first few weeks of pregnancy, results in damage to the vertebrae and spinal cord. By the fourth week of gestation, one or more vertebrae fail to fuse to protect the spinal cord; instead, the spinal cord and its covering membranes bulge out through the spinal column. This bulge may occur anywhere between the skull and the lowest parts of the vertebrae. The protruding sac is surgically placed within the spinal column, a procedure which sometimes results in neurological damage. The effects, obvious at birth, may range from mild to severe. A child with mild spina bifida may have no physical signs or a clump of hair covering the area of the cleft. The effects of severe spina bifida may be paralysis, loss of sensation in the lower limbs, incontinence, and kidney problems. Environmental and hereditary factors are thought to cause spina bifida. Most children with spina bifida have no cognitive defects and are educated along with their peers in regular classrooms.

### Muscular dystrophy

Muscular dystrophy is an inherited condition characterized by a progressive degeneration of the muscles. At birth, the child appears to be developing normally, but for an unknown reason the muscle fibres begin to break down and are replaced by fatty tissues. Children with Duchenne's muscular dystrophy have limbs that appear normal; however, there is significant weakening leading to an inability to walk in middle or late childhood. This progressive muscle weakness is associated with death due to pneumonia, exhaustion, or heart failure in adolescence or early adulthood. A second, less common type of muscular dystrophy is Landouzy-Dejerine, which results in weakened facial and shoulder muscles but is not life threatening. No known cure for muscular dystrophy exists.

## How to Help Students with Physical Disabilities

To make students feel welcome, ensure that the classroom furniture is arranged to accommodate the mobility aids, such as crutches, walker, or wheelchair. Make yourself familiar with specialized equipment, such as pencil holders, book holders, page turners, or special desks, and ensure that there is a place to store the equipment in the classroom. Assign any student with a physical disability a locker in a convenient location and ensure that he knows where the elevator and ramp are located.

Since the student may miss school for medical reasons, provide work to be done at home and evaluate it. If necessary, reduce the amount of work during the absences. As well, try to keep in touch by e-mail, telephone, or letters. When the child returns, inquire about any side effects of medication, for example, fatigue.

The student probably will not require many special accommodations. Assuming that there are no learning difficulties or developmental disability, the student may need only extra time for tests, exams, and assignments. If there is no behavioral disorder, the student should be expected to follow the classroom rules and to accept the same consequences for misbehavior as other members of the class.

However, you can probably help the student in the area of social acceptance. Model accepting behavior and with the student's permission, discuss the disability with the class. Plan group work using cooperative learning techniques and ensure that the student can succeed at the assigned task. For pair work, select someone who is tolerant and well liked to work with the student who has the disability. To further socializing, encourage the student to become involved in extracurricular activities, such as the school newspaper, yearbook, or a club. When it comes to the student's toileting needs and routines, ensure privacy, and if required, arrange for the help of the teacher aide.

## Understand Your Students' Disabilities

As this chapter suggests, working with students who have these low-incidence disabilities is not difficult. The key ideas are to be knowledgeable about the disabilities of your students, their specific strengths and needs, and any specialized equipment. Be sure to communicate regularly with the students, their parents, and others working with the students, too. Finally, show a positive attitude and a willingness to make accommodations that will permit the students to experience success in your classroom.

# Appendices

# Screening Checklist

Name: _____ Grade: _____ Date of Birth: _____

**Language**

❑ Oral Reading

❑ Reading Comprehension

❑ Spelling

❑ Written Expression

❑ Oral Expression

❑ Oral Comprehension

**Math**

❑ Concepts

❑ Facts

❑ Problem Solving

**Motor Skills**

❑ Fine Motor

❑ Gross Motor

**Work Skills**

❑  Organization

❑  Attention Span

❑  Social Skills

**Other**

**Summary**

# Planning Sheet

Name: _____ Date: _____

Grade: _____

**Strengths**                                            **Weaknesses**

**Goals**

**Adaptations**

**Post-Implementation Results**

**Decision**

# Novel Study Form

Name: _____

Novel: _____

**Setting:**


**Main Characters:**



**Plot:**

1. Introduction


2. Rising Action




3. Climax


4. Falling Action


5. Resolution

# Story Planner

Name: _____

Title: _____

**Introduction** (Include where and when the story takes place, who the main characters are, and briefly what is happening):

**Action** (Describe the problem or conflict and how the main character handled it):

**Resolution** (Tell how the problem or conflict was resolved):

# Frame for Writing a Five-Paragraph Essay

**Essay Title:** _____

**Introduction** (Present your thesis or main purpose or focus.): _____

_____

_____

**Body** (After noting your ideas, prioritize them from 1 to 3 with 1 being the strongest and 3 being the weakest. Write your essay so that 2 is presented first, followed by 3 and 1 — save the strongest to the last.):

Idea: _____

Supporting Points: _____

_____

_____

Idea: _____

Supporting Points: _____

_____

_____

Strongest Idea: _____

Supporting Points: _____

_____

_____

**Conclusion:** _____

_____

_____

# "COPS" Strategy

Title of Work: _____

The COPS strategy provides a way for the reader to look at a person's written work and check that the writer has observed key rules and conventions that apply to writing. Review the work with each criterion in mind, and then make check marks on the editorial summary chart below, where appropriate.

*Capitalization:* Does a capital letter appear at the beginning of each sentence and as the first letter of every proper noun?

*Overall Appearance:* Is the work neat and formatted attractively?

*Punctuation:* Have all the rules for punctuation been followed?

*Spelling:* Are all the words spelled correctly?

|       | C | O | P | S |
|-------|---|---|---|---|
| Self  |   |   |   |   |
| Peer  |   |   |   |   |
| Adult |   |   |   |   |

# Personal Enrichment Exploration

Focus Topic or Question:

_____

_____

What Was Learned:

_____

_____

_____

_____

_____

_____

_____

_____

Other Topics or Questions That Arose:

_____

_____

Resources Consulted (Books, Internet, People, etc.):

_____

_____

_____

_____

# Learning Contract for Independent Study

Title of Project: _____

Description of Project (Include the purpose and the process for gathering data.):

_____

_____

_____

_____

_____

_____

_____

Type of Product (Describe what will be produced.):

_____

_____

Criteria for Evaluation:

_____

_____

Breakdown of Marks:

_____

_____

Due Date: _____

_____          _____
Signature of Student and Date                        Signature of Teacher and Date

# References

American Association on Mental Retardation. (1993). *Mental retardation: Definition, classification, and systems of support* (9th ed.). Washington, DC: Author.

American Psychiatric Association. (1994). *Diagnostic and statistical manual of mental disorders* (4th ed.). Washington, DC: Author.

Bloom, B. S. (Ed.). (1956). *Taxonomy of educational objectives: Handbook 1: Cognitive domain.* New York: David McKay.

British Columbia Ministry of Education, Skills & Training. (1995). *Awareness of chronic health conditions.* Victoria, BC: Queen's Printer for British Columbia.

Colvin. G., Ainge, D., & Nelson, R. (1997). How to defuse confrontations. *Teaching Exceptional Children, 29* (6), 47–51.

Dreikurs, R., & Cassel, P. (1992). *Discipline without tears* (2nd ed.). New York: Plume.

Gardner, H. (1983). *Frames of mind.* New York: Basic Books.

Gordon, T. (1974*). T.E.T. — Teacher Effectiveness Training.* New York: Peter H. Wyden.

Johns, B., & Carr, V. (1995). *Techniques for managing verbally and physically aggressive students.* Denver, CO: Love.

Kintsch, E. (1990). Macroprocesses and microprocesses in the development of summarization skill. *Cognition and Instruction, 7,* 161–195.

Lyon, G. (1995). Research initiatives in learning disabilities: Contributions from scientists supported by the National Institutes of Child Health and Human Development. *Journal of Child Neurology, 10* (1), 5120–5126.

Renzulli, J. (1979). *What makes giftedness: A reexamination of the definition of the gifted and talented.* Ventura, CA: Ventura County Superintendent of Schools Office.

Schumacker, J. B., Deshler, D. D., Nolan, S., Clark, F. L., Alley, G. R., & Warren, M. M. (1981). *Error monitoring strategy: A learning strategy for improving academic performance of LD adolescents.* (Research Report No. 32). Lawrence, KS: University of Kansas IRLD.

Schumaker, J. B., Deshler, D. D., Alley, G. R., & Denton, D. H. (1982). Multipass: A learning strategy for improving comprehension. *Learning Disability Quarterly, 5,* 295–304.

Smith, T., Polloway, E., Dowdy, C., & Blalock, G. (1997). *Children and adults with learning disabilities.* Boston: Allyn and Bacon.

# Index